Publisher: Pierre-Marie Dumont
Editors: Romain Lizé, Narthex (French Bishop Conference)
Assistants to the editor: Isabelle Mascaras, Pascale van de Walle

Editor for hymns: Pr. Anthony Esolen
Translation: Janet Chevrier
Copyediting: Andrew Matt

Art Direction: Élisabeth Hébert
Layout: Élise Borel
Iconography: Isabelle Mascaras
Production: Sabine Marioni
Photo engraving: Aquatre

ISBN: 978-1-936260-70-6
First edition: July 2013

www.magnificat.com

Splendors of the Creed

Fr. Joseph T. Lienhard, s.j.
Meditations

Fr. Frédéric Curnier-Laroche
Art Commentaries

Magnificat

Paris • New York • Oxford • Madrid

Table of Contents

Credo in unum Deum,
Patrem omnipotentem,
factorem caeli et terrae,
visibilium omnium et invisibilium.

Et in unum Dominum Iesum Christum,
Filium Dei unigenitum,
et ex Patre natum ante omnia saecula.
Deum de Deo, lumen de lumine,
Deum verum de Deo vero,
genitum, non factum, consubstantialem Patri:
per quem omnia facta sunt.
Qui propter nos homines et propter nostram salutem
descendit de caelis.
Et incarnatus est de Spiritu Sancto ex Maria Virgine,
et homo factus est.

Crucifixus etiam pro nobis sub Pontio Pilato,
passus et sepultus est,
et resurrexit tertia die,
secundum Scripturas,
et ascendit in caelum,
sedet ad dexteram Patris.
Et iterum venturus est cum gloria,
judicare vivos et mortuos,
cujus regni non erit finis.

Et in Spiritum Sanctum, Dominum et vivificantem:
qui ex Patre Filioque procedit;
qui cum Patre et Filio, simul adoratur et conglorificatur:
qui locutus est per prophetas.

Et unam, sanctam, catholicam et apostolicam Ecclesiam.
Confiteor unum baptisma in remissionem peccatorum.
Et exspecto resurrectionem mortuorum,
et vitam venturi saeculi.
Amen.

I believe in one God,
the Father almighty,
maker of heaven and earth,
of all things visible and invisible.

I believe in one Lord Jesus Christ,
the Only Begotten Son of God,
born of the Father before all ages.
God from God, Light from Light,
true God from true God,
begotten, not made, consubstantial with the Father;
through him all things were made.
For us men and for our salvation
he came down from heaven,
and by the Holy Spirit was incarnate of the Virgin Mary,
and became man.

For our sake he was crucified under Pontius Pilate,
he suffered death and was buried,
and rose again on the third day
in accordance with the Scriptures.
He ascended into heaven
and is seated at the right hand of the Father.
He will come again in glory
to judge the living and the dead
and his kingdom will have no end.

I believe in the Holy Spirit, the Lord, the giver of life,
who proceeds from the Father and the Son,
who with the Father and the Son is adored and glorified,
who has spoken through the prophets.

I believe in one, holy, catholic and apostolic Church.
I confess one Baptism for the forgiveness of sins
and I look forward to the resurrection of the dead
and the life of the world to come.
Amen.

Foreword

Pierre-Marie Dumont
Publisher of Magnificat
President of the Magnificat Foundation

Any pilgrim fortunate enough to participate in the liturgy in Rome's Saint Peter's Square, amid the colorful crowds of the faithful, experiences an almost physical sensation of belonging to the one, holy, catholic, and apostolic Church. The place itself radiates this very particular grace. To celebrate one's faith in the exact spot where Saint Peter founded his universal ministry and was martyred is not without effect. In no other place in the world is the power of the apostolic succession so palpable. This blessing of the communion of faith is embodied in the majestic beauty of Bernini's colonnade (see illustration, pages 96-97) and by the truly "corporeal" impression created by these two semi-circular wings spread out to embrace the city and the world. This is no lucky happenstance: the artist who designed this architectural masterpiece specifically wished to evoke the two great arms of our holy Mother Church gathering to her heart the people of the new and eternal covenant.

By way of introduction to this volume, I'd like to let you in on a secret, something that happened to me right there in Rome during the Year of Faith. On this particular occasion, I was blessed enough to take part in the celebration of Mass in Saint Peter's Square, one pilgrim among many in the middle of an immense crowd, a crowd from all nations, races, peoples, and tongues. We were all standing facing the altar of the Holy Sacrifice, the source of our salvation. Just at the moment when the chant of the Creed filled the air, it was as though my heart, already stirred by the proclamation of the Word of God, began to burn within me. With that, Bernini's colonnade, resplendent in the paschal light of Rome's golden sunshine, appeared to me like a manifestation, symbolic but intensely expressive, of the Church's Profession of Faith. And so, as we sang, "*Et unam, sanctam, catholicam et apostolicam Ecclesiam,*" it was truly in the arms of the Church, *Mater et Magistra*, that in that Year of Faith I became conscious of my belonging. I became aware that, like Bernini's colonnade, the Creed marks a border, a frontier showing you where you stand: inside or out—of Saint Peter's Square in the first case, and of the Church in the second. But I could clearly see that this frontier wasn't a wall. Like Bernini's colonnade, the Creed demarcates a space of freedom: an enclosure that is solid yet transparent, solemn yet welcoming, majestic yet open to all.

I still recall how each and every one of the columns, standing solid and upright like boundary markers planted deep in the earth by heaven itself, seemed to me like so many symbols of the truths of the faith professed in the Creed. For is not each article of our faith a rock solid foundation from which the treasures of truth and life can eternally bear fruit? This is what is truly expressed in the one hundred and forty Baroque statues that enliven the strict rigidity of the columns. Through the articles of faith, Christian life is built upon bedrock, but it is the witness of the faithful that gives these monolithic articles spirit and life. And so, underpinning our contemplation of the Creed, Bernini offers a forest of hieratic shafts, their capitals reaching up into the life-giving wind of the Spirit—but it was a living and active faith that gave forms and faces to this throng of martyrs, of Fathers and Doctors of the Church, of holy saints who, through their lives and their deaths, defended and glorified the fruitfulness of Truth. This entire monumental litany of friends of God and servants of man is the visual illustration of a teaching of Pope Benedict XVI: "Having faith in the Lord is not something that solely involves our intelligence, the area of intellectual knowledge; rather, it is a change that involves our life, our whole self: feelings, heart, intelligence, will, corporeity, emotions and human relationships. With faith everything truly changes, in us and for us, and our future destiny is clearly revealed, the truth of our vocation in history, the meaning of life, the pleasure of being pilgrims bound for the heavenly Homeland" (General Audience, October 17, 2012).

This beautiful book will offer countless occasions for readers—and art lovers too!—to share in this spiritual experience of the splendor of truth. Here you will discover with wonder how, throughout the life of the Church, inspired writers and artists have placed their own particular genius at the service of the expression of Christian faith. They have left a rich and original legacy to all people of good will who wish to rediscover the joy of believing. In

Page 4:
The First Council of Nicea*, Novgorod School (late 15th century),*
tempera on wood, 9 x 11 in.

In the Anatolian city of Nicea represented at the top of the painting, the bishops, clothed in red and gold, are convened by Emperor Constantine and formulate the confession of faith shared in common by the entire Church. Gathered around the throne, some hold Holy Scriptures, while others, in the lower register, debate the heresy of the priest Arius, who denied the divinity of Christ. To the left we behold the dream of a bishop: under a purple baldaquin, Jesus, in the guise of the young "Emmanuel" (God-is-with-us) prophesied by Isaiah (7:14), displays his rent garment, symbol of the threatening schism he wished to avoid. Following the inspired words of the first ecumenical council of the Church, let us now enter into the heart of the profession that unites us in one and the same faith.

this sense, *Splendors of the Creed* is a fitting response to the words Pope Francis, then-Cardinal Bergoglio, addressed to priests in his homily for the Chrism Mass on April 21, 2011: "We are sent to preach the truth, to do good to all, and to bring joy to our people. [But] it is not enough that our truth is orthodox and our pastoral action effective. Without the joy of beauty, truth becomes merciless, cold, and arrogant."

At a time when Catholicism suffers from both its own frailty as well as caricatures in the media, this volume will have the effect of a soothing balm on the Christian soul. Above all, its pages offer to each and every one the opportunity to refresh their faith through these noble reflections on the Creed in the words and images of our forebears. But this book is anything but nostalgia for a bygone age. On the contrary, it calls on us to draw deeply from the treasure trove of our ancient and ever young Christian heritage—the better to invite us in the here and now to contemplate, celebrate, and profess the Catholic Faith handed down to us by the Apostles, the better to witness to it before the world, that the long chain of the transmission of the faith may go unbroken from generation to generation—"For I handed on to you as of first importance what I also received: that Christ died for our sins in accordance with the scriptures; that he was buried; that he was raised on the third day in accordance with the scriptures" (1 Cor 15:3-4). May our generation not be that weak link which brought our Lord Jesus Christ to ask: "But when the Son of Man comes, will he find faith on earth?" (Lk 18:8). . .

In order to hand on the tradition, we must dare to give a confident, vibrant account of our faith, but—that is not enough—we must also live it with fervor. For, it is true, "If I have all faith so as to move mountains but do not have love, I am nothing" (1 Cor 13:2)! ■

Faith

Faith makes me anything, or all
That I believe is in the sacred story,
And where sin placeth me in Adam's fall,
Faith sets me higher in his glory.

If I go lower in the book,
What can be lower than the common manger?
Faith puts me there with Him, who sweetly took
Our flesh and frailty, death and danger.

If bliss had lain in art or strength,
None but the wise or strong had gained it;
Where now by Faith all arms are of a length;
One size doth all conditions fit.

What though my body run to dust?
Faith cleaves unto it, counting every grain
With an exact and most particular trust,
Reserving all for flesh again.

George Herbert
From "Faith"

CREDO

God our Father,
who by sending into the world
the Word of truth and the Spirit of sanctification
made known to the human race your wondrous mystery,
grant us, we pray, that in professing the true faith,
we may acknowledge the Trinity of eternal glory
and adore your Unity, powerful in majesty.

A creed is a confession of Christian faith, expressed in fixed words. Liturgically, its home is the sacrament of baptism. In the early Church, before a candidate was baptized, he was asked to profess his faith—that is, before baptism was administered the one to be baptized had to recite the Creed.

The oldest Christian Creed is also the simplest: "Jesus is Lord," three words in English, two in Saint Paul's Greek. The Apostle tells us that we can profess this faith only with the help of God; he writes, "I want you to understand that no one speaking by the Spirit of God ever says 'Jesus be cursed!' and no one can say 'Jesus is Lord' except by the Holy Spirit" (1 Cor 12:3). In another epistle he writes, "If you confess with your lips that Jesus is Lord and believe in your heart that God raised him from the dead, you will be saved" (Rom 10:9). The whole of Christian faith is contained in this one confession, "Jesus is Lord," and the martyrs were willing to die for these words.

The oldest witness to the baptismal Creed is Hippolytus of Rome who, around the year 215, wrote an intriguing work called the *Apostolic Tradition*. Hippolytus vividly describes the rite of baptism: the candidate and a deacon step down into the baptismal font, while the bishop kneels at the edge of the font. The bishop asks three questions: "Do you believe in God, the Father Almighty?" "Do you believe in Jesus Christ, the Son of God. . .?" "Do you believe in the Holy Spirit in the holy Church?" After each question, the candidate states, "I believe," and the bishop immerses him in the water. Thus the Creed is trinitarian: belief in one God whose name is Father, Son, and Holy Spirit.

In the year 325 an extraordinary event took place. A dispute had arisen among Christians about the Son: was the Son truly God, or merely the first and greatest of all God's creatures? To resolve the dispute, the Emperor Constantine

Previous page:
Master Honoré (imitator of), ***The Apostles' Creed*** *(1295)*
miniature, 7.6 x 5.2 in.

"How the Apostles make the creed." What better way to introduce us into the very heart of this gathering than with the artist's own opening inscription at the top of this illuminated manuscript. Here is a veritable council in which each participant points an exaggeratedly long finger at the core of the profession of faith: "I believe in one God." This already powerful gesture is accentuated by the presence of the Holy Spirit who, bursting forth from the clouds in the upper register, seems to ratify this collegial declaration of faith and bless the Apostles, assembled in a space rendered by Gothic vaulting. The Apostles, almost all of advanced age with flourishing beards—a symbol of wisdom—are dressed in voluminous robes of alternating colors to create an impression of depth.
Let us enter now with the Twelve into the heart of our faith. And not only with them, but with all those who have pronounced these words with confidence and joy—together we are a great throng!

convoked the Council of Nicea, the first ecumenical council. The bishops at the council—there were about three hundred—were determined to teach the true faith. They did not issue a long theological tract, nor did they simply condemn some errors. Instead, they took a basic baptismal creed, added a few key phrases, and made it their own. Thus they stated that there is only one faith, and the simple faith of a candidate for baptism is the same faith as the faith of three hundred bishops assembled in council. And it is our faith, too.

The Creed that we will ponder in these meditations is often called the Nicene Creed, the Creed of the Council of Nicea or, by a somewhat awkward title, the Niceno-Constantinopolitan Creed. But in fact it is the Creed of the Council of Constantinople, the second ecumenical council, which took place in 381.

This Creed is one that we should love and treasure. It has an extended treatment of the Holy Spirit, which the Creed of Nicea does not. And it is the most ecumenical document of Christianity after the New Testament. Latin-rite Catholics profess it at Mass every Sunday and on every solemn feast throughout the year. Byzantine-rite Christians profess it during every Divine Liturgy. And many other Christians accept its authority. Several times, Pope John Paul II stood next to the head of another Christian church in Saint Peter's basilica, and they professed the Creed of Constantinople together. The power of this gesture should not be missed: at the very heart of our Christian faith, we are one. Each Sunday, as we profess this faith, our hearts should soar, as we are united with Christians of the past sixteen centuries, united with Christians throughout the world on that day, united with all Christians who will live until the end of time.

And so we say, "I believe in one God. . . ."

God Saw That It Was Good

These are Thy glorious works, Parent of good,
Almighty, Thine this universal frame,
Thus wondrous fair; Thyself how wondrous then!
Unspeakable, who sit'st above these Heavens
To us invisible or dimly seen
In these thy lowest works, yet these declare
Thy goodness beyond thought, and Power Divine:
Speak ye who best can tell, ye Sons of Light,
Angels, for ye behold Him, and with songs
And choral symphonies, Day without Night,
Circle His throne rejoicing, ye in Heaven;
On Earth join all ye Creatures to extol
Him first, Him last, Him midst, and without end

John Milton
From *Paradise Lost*
The morning prayer of Adam and Eve

Credo in unum Deum

I believe in one God, the Father almighty,
maker of heaven and earth,
of all things visible and invisible.

O All-Transcendent God
(and what other name could describe you?),
what words can hymn your praises?
No word does you justice.
What mind can probe your secret?
No mind can encompass you.

Previous page:
Girolamo dai Libri (c. 1474-1555), ***God the Father with His Hand Raised in Blessing***
pen, brown ink and wash, with white on cream highlights,
paper on wood panel backing 2.7 x 3.2 in.

God leans down toward us—he, the Almighty, shining in glory, as rays of light flow out from his triangular halo, reminding us that he is one God in three persons. The unfathomable mystery quietly reveals itself through this delicate, somewhat subdued figure—no doubt an effect of the fragile texture of this painting on wood marked by the passage of time. How can God be represented? Impossible, as the Decalogue advises us. Conforming to an ancient though far from satisfactory tradition, iconographical convention adopted the image of an old man. Throughout the ages, artists have sought a way to evoke the eternal nature of the One who is beyond time, who is its beginning and its end. Since we have seen Christ, the incarnate Son, we have seen the Father (Jn 14:9)—such was the source that enabled Christian art to circumvent the prohibition: "You shall not carve idols for yourselves in the shape of anything in the sky above" (Ex 20:4). It remains for us, through our lives and our faith, to inscribe our name in the Book of Life he holds out to us.

Philippe de Champaigne (1602-1674), ***God the Father Creating the Material Universe*** *(c. 1633), oil on canvas, 86.6 x 69 in.*

It is the essence of divinity itself that the French Baroque artist offers in this delicate painting imbued with spirituality. A warm, gentle glow bathes the entire composition, which highlights the Creator surging forth from the clouds. Champaigne presents God the almighty Father, the source of the universe, here depicted by the sphere on which he rests his left hand. We, mere mortals limited within the confines of space and time, are urged to join in the adoration of the celestial choir. Though in reality invisible, through the artist's brush the multitude of angels is revealed here as a band of pearly-faced eternal youths. At the invitation of the pink-robed angel staring tenderly at us, we too add our voices to their song of acclamation which the little cherub points out on the unfurled scroll—"Gloria in excelsis." Faith and prayer allow this unending miracle of immersion in contemplation and praise, of participation in this invisible universe. How can we not be moved by this elegant, meticulous brushwork, this multi-media meditation in which light and music intertwine, intangible, and yet, like God the Creator, made accessible to us in radiant color?

"I believe." The Creed is a profession of faith. By its nature, it is a public profession. In the early Church, candidates for baptism stood up before the Christian community and recited the Creed. Saint Augustine, in his *Confessions*, tells the story of a great rhetorician and philosopher, Marius Victorinus, who for most of his life worshiped idols and vehemently defended idolatry. In his later years, he came to accept Christian faith and eventually asked for baptism. The clergy at Rome, where he was to be baptized, offered to spare him the embarrassment of a public profession of the Creed; given his age and dignity, they said, he could make the profession privately. But Marius said, No. For many years I taught falsehood and lies in public; now I will profess the truth in public. And a great man became a Christian that day.

What is our faith? We believe in one God, and in one God only. And God is not some distant, isolated being, concerned only with itself and its perfections, as some Greek philosophers said.

Maurice Denis (1870-1943), ***Young Girls and Angels,*** *(1908) oil on canvas, 43.7 x 41.3 in.*

In his decor of Eternal Spring, an ensemble linking images of sacred and profane springtime in the month of Mary, Maurice Denis remains faithful to the traditional representation of these winged spiritual beings. In the gentle cool of early dawn, angels shower the earth with a rain of flowers. Let us be filled anew with sensations of sweetness and light as, amid the tender green of budding foliage, the ethereal nature of these angels bears the same message of hope, peace, and salvation that they proclaimed to the humble shepherds in Bethlehem.

No, God is a person, and he is related to us in the closest way possible; he is the one we call Father: one God, the Father. And he is almighty or, as the Greeks call him, Pantokrator, the Ruler of All.

And God is maker, creator. At this point, the Creed takes out a kind of insurance. In the Hebrew Old Testament, the expression for "the whole world" is "heaven and earth." In Greek thought, it is "all things visible and invisible." In other words, the Creed says that, no matter how you look at it, God made all things. There are only two ways to exist: to be God, or to be made by God. There is nothing that is not either God or made by him.

This statement has profound consequences. Because God is all-good, all that he makes participates in his goodness, just as it participates in his being. And God is all-wise and all-beautiful; all that he makes participates in some way in his wisdom and in his beauty. Perhaps it is easier to see God's goodness and beauty in the sun and the moon, in great mountains and placid lakes, in a rose and in the song of a bird, than in a mosquito or a cockroach. But somehow, they too participate in God's attributes. The principle stands: all that God makes is true, good, and beautiful, each in its own way. We affirm that the world we live in, despite all our confusion and doubt and suffering, participates in some mysterious way in God's being and goodness and beauty and wisdom.

God cannot make evil because, we may say, he does not have it in him. This is not to deny that evil exists; but evil is not there

Next page:
The Dome of the Creation *(1215-1235),*
narthex mosaic, San Marco Basilica, Venice, Italy

This splendid example of Venetian mosaic encompasses the creation story in twenty-five episodes drawn from the Book of Genesis. Each day of creation takes place in the presence of angels who assist God. This series of scenes presents the Creator in the form of a young, beardless Christ, in keeping with an ancient tradition still current among these thirteenth-century mosaicists. He is clothed in a gilded cloak and bears a cruciform scepter in his left hand, both attributes of sovereignty. Day follows day in this luminous and colorful cycle, beginning with the striking image of the Spirit hovering over chaos (at center).

VLAVDATVOCES
PROMENDOSERE
DENTCHERVBI
NCRISTIFLAMA

because God created it. It exists because of the free choice of creatures. But if evil entered the world through free choice, it can ultimately be abolished by free choice.

I believe in God, the Father, maker of all things. With these words we stake out our basic outlook on life, and that outlook is confident and serene. Others may see the world as a battleground between two forces, light and darkness, or as a place where unintelligibility exists at the very root of things. But we Christians know that God is superior to all the evil that we cause, and that, finally, everything will make sense, even if we do not understand it now. As Saint Paul says so beautifully, "For now we see in a mirror dimly, but then face to face. Now I know in part; then I shall understand fully" (1 Cor 13:12).

Saint Gregory Nazianzen, one of the great theologians of the ancient Greek church, was a student in Athens, along with his friend, Saint Basil of Caesarea. In a funeral oration for Basil, Gregory described their goal: "Different men have different names, derived from their fathers, their families, their pursuits, their exploits; we had but one great business and name—to be and to be called Christians—of which we thought more than" all else that is. To be called Christians, to hear a stranger profess the Creed and to realize that we are not strangers, is a beautiful moment.

Our Creed begins, "I believe," because each individual has received the gift of faith. But on Sunday, we stand together and say, "I believe." Our common Creed unites us; it also sets us apart. We accept truths that others do not; we live in a way that others do not. To say the Creed and mean it is an act that we should reflect on often; to say the Creed and mean it should mark our lives each day. The martyrs died for the Creed; we live for it. Like Marius Victorinus, we should have the courage to profess our faith before all the world. ■

Auguste Rodin (1840-1917), ***The Hand of God*** *or* ***Creation*** *(c. 1896), marble, 30.7 x 21.2 x 37 in.*

An extraordinary process of artistic creation plays a fundamental and edifying role here. We are witnesses of a veritable birth: the birth of the human species through the creative action of God. All of Rodin's genius is on display here, for he succeeds in capturing this divine act in the form of a rough-hewn block of marble from which emerge the polished and entwined figures of the first man and woman. This primordial pair is simultaneously fashioned, held, and caressed by the monumental divine hand, itself stretching up from the inchoate mass of the base. As we do a turn around this sculpture, in step with the dance of life it depicts, one after another aspect of the piece reveals itself from each different standpoint. The play of light and shadow transfigures this hand which, through its anatomical detail, seems to throb with a living pulse. It almost beckons us to run our fingers over these two figures welling up with a life force that fills and animates their young bodies as though for the first time. Let us celebrate the miracle of such art which ennobles material at the service of incarnation, while at the same time materializing the void and the immaterial.

The Word That Speaks the World

"And Thou my Word, begotten Son, by Thee
This I perform, speak Thou, and be it done;
My overshadowing Spirit and might with Thee
I send along, ride forth, and bid the Deep
Within appointed bounds be Heaven and Earth,
Boundless the Deep, because I am who fill
Infinitude, nor vacuous the space."

So spake the Almighty, and to what He spake
His Word, the Filial Godhead, gave effect. . .
. . .The Son
On His great Expedition now appeared,
Girt with Omnipotence, with Radiance crowned
Of Majesty Divine, Sapience and Love
Immense, and all His Father in Him shone.

John Milton
From *Paradise Lost*

Et in unum Dominum Iesum Christum

I believe in one Lord Jesus Christ,
the Only Begotten Son of God,
born of the Father before all ages.
God from God, Light from Light,
true God from true God,
begotten, not made, consubstantial with the Father;
through him all things were made.

And you so loved the world,
Father most holy,
that in the fullness of time
you sent your Only Begotten Son to be our Savior.

Previous page:
Christ in Majesty Surrounded by Symbols of the Evangelists *(c. 1400)*
illumination, 9.3 x 7 in.

Standing out to beautiful effect against a scarlet damask background, Jesus is represented as the one Lord, enthroned and holding the earthly sphere in his hand. He is the Only Begotten Son of God, haloed and giving his blessing, clad in a magnificent cloak of blue. Beyond time and with no spatial point of reference, with nothing precisely to identify the setting, the person of the Son is consubstantial with the Father in their shared divine nature. Their unique identity is reinforced by a series of significant details: Christ is framed, on the left, by a small altar bearing the symbol of the Eucharist (the chalice and the host), and, on the right, by the tablets of the Law. The tetramorph, the four symbols of the Evangelists, surrounds the throne of God. These four living creatures have their source in the Book of Revelation (4:6-8) and were attributed by the Fathers of the Church to the Evangelists: the lion for Mark, the ox for Luke, the man or angel for Matthew, and the eagle for John.

The Wissembourg Head of Christ *(c. 1060)*
stained glass, diameter 9.8 in.

He looks at me. More than that: he is staring at me. And I have no choice but to look back in turn, struck, fascinated by his large eyes and ready to plunge into the depths of his intense gaze. The beauty of the created is united with the Uncreated. I am before stained glass that turns light into matter. The light shining through the glass lends it a kind of holiness and spiritual clarity. Without the light, it would be nothing. God is the light of all that is. Without his creative light, nothing would exist. The Light is the first principle of the cosmos and existence. "The true light, which enlightens everyone, was coming into the world. . .and the world came to be through him" (Jn 1:9-10). I affirm this in the Creed. This Christ, Light from Light, is a symbol of Illumination. Christian art is a manifestation of this closeness, this intimacy that the risen Christ seems to elicit in this encounter he establishes between us. Who ever dared suggest that the Middle Ages were characterized by obscurantism and fear? If such were the case, I would never be able to respond to the invitation I am offered here of receiving, through contemplation of this work, the only Son of God, haloed in delicate azure as a reminder of his divine origin.

To fully appreciate the Creed, we need to consider its structure. Like all eastern creeds, the Creed of Constantinople, in the second article, speaks of the Lord Jesus Christ in two steps: first, of the eternal Son of God and of his relation to God the Father, and then of the Son of Man: his Incarnation and birth, his death and Resurrection, his Ascension and second coming.

This article of the Creed begins with a title: "one Lord Jesus Christ." The name Jesus is the Lord's human name. It is another form of the name Joshua, and it means "God saves." Saint Matthew's Gospel tells us that an angel of the Lord appeared to Saint Joseph in a dream and said to him, about the child whom Mary his betrothed had conceived, "she will bear a son, and you shall call his name Jesus, for he will save his people from their sins" (Mt 1:21). By his very name, therefore, Jesus is designated as our Savior.

The next part of the phrase, "Christ," is a title. It means "the Anointed," and it is the Greek form of the Hebrew Messiah. To anoint someone with oil was a sacrament, in the broad sense: a sign with added meaning. In the ancient world, to be anointed with oil, especially perfumed oil, was a sign of luxury. In the Old Testament, three sorts of people received their office by anointing: priests, prophets, and kings. And Jesus the Christ is all three: the High Priest of the new covenant, the prophet like Moses (see Dt 18:15), and the King of the Universe who reigned from the cross.

And finally, "Lord" is a title of divinity, a designation that Jesus is God. The Creed speaks of one Lord, and there is no other. A fascinating passage from a second-century writing, called the *Martyrdom of Polycarp*, illustrates this conviction beautifully. The aged bishop Polycarp, eighty-six years old, is on trial for his life, because he is a Christian. The judge is, at first, sympathetic to the dignified old man, and he wants to find a way to release Polycarp. The judge asks Polycarp for one small sign of submission: he says to the aged bishop, "What is wrong with saying, 'Caesar is Lord'?" Every Christian who read or heard those words knew immediately what was wrong with saying "Caesar is Lord": to say "Caesar is Lord" is to deny that Jesus is Lord, for there is only one Lord, Jesus Christ.

Thus, the phrase that begins this part of the Creed already affirms the full truth about Christ: he is true God, the Lord; he is true man, Jesus; and he is the Messiah, the anointed one sent by God as Savior, the Christ.

When this part of the Creed was composed, the faith was threatened by Arianism, which taught that the Son was the first and greatest of all God's creatures, but still a creature and not divine, and surely not equal in being to the Father.

The Creed rejects Arianism in several phrases. First, it insists that the Son is begotten—that is, he comes from the Father's being, not from his will, as creatures do. "Begotten, not made" reinforces the same point. Moreover, his begetting is eternal, "born of the Father before all ages," as the Creed puts it; his existence had no beginning.

The equality of Father and Son is expressed in three parallel phrases: "God from God, Light from Light, true God from true God": the Son is, in every way, all that the Father is save Father.

The Creed also speaks of the Lord Jesus Christ as consubstantial with the Father. The word "consubstantial" is an unfamiliar one, and it has caused some consternation. But the Greek word that it translates also caused some consternation when it was first inserted into the Creed. The word was *homoousios*, from the Greek words *homos*, "same," and *ousia*, "being." The bishops at the Council of Nicea were searching for an expression that would describe the Son's relation to the Father. They had already taken over the creedal formula, "God from God, Light from Light." Now they introduced *homoousios*, a word that had not appeared in any older creed. What they meant by this word can be expressed simply: the Son is God in exactly the

*William Holman Hunt (1827-1910), **The Light of the World** (1851-1853)*
oil on canvas, 49.2 x 23.6 in., Oxford, Keble College

Hanging in the chapel of an Oxford college, this canvas depicts Jesus about to knock on a door long closed and overgrown with weeds—an illustration of the words spoken in the Book of Revelation: "Behold, I stand at the door and knock" (Rv 3:20). The door in the painting has no doorknob and, consequently, can only be opened from the inside—this is the symbol of an obstinately closed spirit. It is a night scene lit principally by the lantern, following a metaphor found in the Psalms: "Your word is a lamp for my feet,/ a light for my path" (Ps 119:105). The weeds suggest our own neglectfulness and accumulated obstructions. The orchard in the background calls to mind the delicious fruits destined for the banquet of the soul. The priestly robe and royal cape worn by this monumental Christ, solid and living for all eternity, are the signs of his reign over the body and soul of those who receive him. He comes to awaken us, to shake us. Is it twilight or dawn we spy behind the trees? The combination of light sources is handled with great mastery; the figure of Jesus appears like a star guiding us through the darkest moments of our lives. The lantern he carries—the light of Truth, light of the divine Word (for Christ is Light, born of the Light)—provides the main source of illumination of the door and weeds in the foreground. The Savior is the promise of a new day and a new life if we welcome him into the heart of our lives, and awaken our slumbering souls to his presence.

same way that the Father is. In other words, there is only one way to be God, and in God there cannot be higher or lower, greater or lesser.

The heart of the issue is salvation. We were lost, and we could not save ourselves. No creature could save us, but only God. Arianism represented one of the last efforts to shape Christianity by Greek philosophy, speculating about the great chain of being. Saint Athanasius of Alexandria, in his life-long opposition to Arianism, set Christian thought on the right course: only God can save us; hence, Christ our Savior must be true God. It followed from this faith that Mary may be called Theotokos, "God-bearer" or "Mother of God," a title Athanasius loved and defended.

Then, in a phrase that merits reflection, we profess that

Anonymous (c. 1100-1160), ***The Son Enthroned***
illuminated miniature, 3.6 x 3.8 in.

"The Lord says to you, my lord:/ 'Take your throne at my right hand,/ while I make your enemies your footstool'" (Ps 110:1). This promise from the Father to the Son is here fulfilled. They are seated together on the same throne. Christ, arrayed in red and azure, receives with gratitude the affectionate gesture of the fatherly hand on his shoulder. Notice that Father and Son are both young. This eternal youthfulness is a mark of the timelessness of divine nature. It underscores as well the profound communion of love and glory that unites them. The Father's halo is red, incandescent like the fire of his love. His Son's blue halo indicates his divinity. The enemies referred to by the Psalmist are placed in a quite uncomfortable position of submission and humiliation. I would rather be in the place of that nice little angel tying up this initial in the form of a circle which, just as the gold background, is a symbol of divine perfection and its infinite nature.

Next page:
Henri Guérin (1929-2009), ***Bursts of Gold*** *(2001)*
stained-glass window, dalle de verre with mineral joints, 24 x 24 in.

Here is a title that truly reflects the work. The explosion of colors and shapes, the juxtaposition of faceted crystals that form this "dalle de verre" stained glass speak to me of my Lord, born "Light from Light." Look how the light brings these shards of glass to life, how it animates this work. Colors participate in this illumination, beginning in the center with cool tones radiating out into warm golden rays. That which cannot be grasped envelops matter—which in turn responds with contrasting shimmers and complementary glints and flashes. The highly varied contours unite in this composition to form a reflection of the brilliance of the One who is "begotten, not made." Henri Guérin reminds us once again that Christian art is an offering to the Light. This stained-glass window, like so many others, is the translucent symbol of eternal day, of the lucidity of contemplation, and the ray of infinte hope. It is the manifestation of the divinity of Christ calling me to live in his presence.

"through him all things were made." The beginning of the Creed states that God is the maker of all things; now we acknowledge that all these things were made through Jesus Christ, the Son. The implications of this clause are profound. The whole meaning of the universe, from its first creation to its final consummation, is to be found in Christ. From its first moments, the world yearned for Christ, and only in Christ is its final meaning to be found: namely, that only in the personal union of the divine and the human in the one Christ do we understand ourselves and our world.

Again and again it comes home to us: our faith is so simple, and yet so profound: one page in a book, the Church's Creed, can direct and guide our entire lives. ■

Omnipotence, in the Manger

Salvation to all that will is nigh;
That All, which always is All everywhere,
Which cannot sin, and yet all sins must bear,
Which cannot die, yet cannot choose but die,

Lo, faithful Virgin, yields Himself to lie
In prison, in thy womb; and though He there
Can take no sin, nor thou give, yet he'll wear
Taken from thence, flesh, which death's force may try.

Ere by the spheres time was created, thou
Wast in His mind, who is thy Son, and Brother;
Whom thou conceiv'st, conceived; yea, thou art now
Thy Maker's maker, and thy Father's mother;

Thou hast light in dark, and shut'st in little room
Immensity cloistered in thy dear womb.

John Donne
"Annunciation"
From *La Corona*

Descendit de caelis

For us men and for our salvation
he came down from heaven,
and by the Holy Spirit was incarnate
of the Virgin Mary, and became man.

O Dayspring,
brightness of eternal Light and Sun of Justice:
come and enlighten those who sit in darkness
and in the shadow of death.

Previous page:
Lorenzo Ghiberti (c. 1378-1455), ***The Annunciation****,*
bronze, 21 x 17.7 in., Florence, Baptistery of Saint John

What virtuosity! What movement! At the heart of the intellectual and spiritual effervescence of the beginning of the Florentine Renaissance, the human form and nature are handled by the artist with a sensitivity and elegance enhanced by gilded highlights. The undulating bodies, the folds of the gowns, the composition of three distinct elements are perfectly integrated within a framework of both sharp angles and curved arches. God the Father, whose face we cannot see, surges forth, releasing the Holy Spirit. At the same time, the angel Gabriel, as light as he is graceful, greets Mary. His feet have not yet touched this earth which, in nine months' time, would know its Savior. His hand, held aloft as he speaks, is directed toward the Virgin. She in turn raises her hand in surprise. This staging of the scene, so full of vitality, reminds us that the Lord wishes to inhabit our daily life. Are we willing, like Mary, standing at the threshold of her own doorstep, to accept the intrusion of God in our lives? Are we ready to give birth to the divine through our faith?

"For us men and for our salvation." What do we mean by salvation? One who needs to be saved was somehow lost. The first chapters of the Book of Genesis describe, in poetic terms, a cosmic event. God created the first human beings in a state of innocence and blessedness. They had free choice, they were tempted, and they fell. Saint Augustine of Hippo sees the heart of the temptation in the serpent's words, "You will be like God" (Gn 2:5). In other words, they sinned by pride, wanting to be what they were not. All sins are sins of pride, wanting to follow ourselves and not God. Because of our first parents' solidarity with all their descendants, all human beings are born in a fallen state, lacking God's grace and marked by original sin.

If the primal sin was pride, it needed to be reversed by humility. So the Creed says, "he came down from heaven." This coming down was not a spatial move, from above to below, so much as it was an act of condescension, expressed so beautifully in a hymn in Saint Paul's letter to the Philippians: "Though he was in the form of God, he did not count

Duccio di Buoninsegna (c. 1255-c. 1318), ***The Nativity*** *(1308-1311)*
tempera on wood, 17 x 17.5 in.

Easily recognizable, this composition is clearly an evocation of the birth of the Savior. And yet, several details invite us to meditate on this moment that changes the very course of human history. The joy of the heavens echoes throughout the earth. All the heavenly host leans toward Jesus, hands opened in postures of prayer, or looks to the sky with gestures of thanksgiving for this gift from God to all the universe. But the drama of the ultimate sacrifice is already present here too. The Virgin lies on a scarlet cushion in the form of a mandorla. She meditates, her fine hands crossing over her heart, as she contemplates her Child. By giving him life, she offers us the Author of Life. There you lie, Jesus, a newborn babe, wrapped not in swaddling but in the future winding-cloths of your shroud. And your cradle looks more like an altar than a manger. This is why your mother contemplates you veiled in sadness. The ox and the ass keep watch over the Child, warming him with their breath. Near Joseph, who sits at a distance meditating upon his mission, the midwives bathe the infant, in keeping with certain apocryphal stories.

equality with God a thing to be grasped, but emptied himself, taking the form of a servant, being born in the likeness of men. And being found in human form he humbled himself and became obedient unto death, even death on a cross" (Phil 2:6–8).

The Creed continues, "and by the Holy Spirit was incarnate of the Virgin Mary." Three words are key here: "Virgin Mary," "Holy Spirit," and "incarnate." The mother of Jesus was a virgin when she conceived him, and remained a virgin all her life. Jesus had a human mother but no human father. As we read in Saint Luke's Gospel, the angel Gabriel said to Mary, "The Holy Spirit will come upon you, and the power of the Most High will overshadow you; therefore the child to be born will be called holy, the Son of God" (Lk 1:35). The Holy Spirit, the third Person of the Blessed Trinity, caused Mary to be fruitful, to conceive a child. The second Person of the Blessed Trinity, by the power of the same Holy Spirit, took flesh in Mary's womb.

And the word "flesh" is key. It is the word contained, in its Latin form, in "incarnation." The flesh of Christ was not some heavenly substance, as some early heretics maintained, or an illusion, as others tried to assert. It was as real and as human as our own bodies, and hence Jesus, in his human nature, was one of us. He was not some third sort of being, between God and man, but true God and true man.

The word "consubstantial," found in this Creed, was used in a marvelous way by the fourth ecumenical council, the Council of Chalcedon, held in 451, to express in concise terms the true divinity and the true humanity of Christ. That council taught that the Lord Jesus Christ is "consubstantial with the Father as regards his

Michelangelo Merisi da Caravaggio (1571-1610)
The Madonna of Loreto *(1603-1605), oil on canvas, 102 x 59 in.*
Rome, Church of Sant'Agostino

Here is a mother presenting her son to us. Wonderful in her calm benevolence, clothed in velvet and silk, full of grace and beauty, but of strength and gravity as well, she bends her pure face down to two pilgrims. Elderly, tired, and poor, they adore and contemplate this apparition on the threshold of a house caressed by a coruscating light. She offers them her compassion but, above all, the one true blessing, she offers the Son of God for our salvation. For is the brilliantly white cloth not already the shroud from which he will rise victorious over sin and death? The infant has grown, has become almost too heavy for Mary to carry, yet she bears him still. God made man is called to grow up and fulfill his mission. Let us dare to enter into this exchange of gazes and gestures, for the emotion of this couple at prayer is our emotion as well. How terribly moving, this old woman, animated by such pure faith, adoring the one who intercedes for her—for us—before God; the rugged beauty of this couple, their faces and hands worn by a life of suffering, but also of hope. Their blackened, calloused feet contrast with those of the Virgin whose toes lightly brush the stone doorstep, as though executing a delicate dance. Do we see here an illustration of Mother and Child come "down from heaven," as the words of the Creed tell us—for they seem to have only just gracefully alighted upon the earth. . .

Youhannès de Berkri, ***The Baptism of Christ*** *(1362)*
illuminated miniature

This illumination from an Armenian manuscript takes us to the turbulent waters of the Jordan, resembling the "living waters" described by Ezekiel. John is baptizing Jesus. Faithful to the Gospel account (Mk 1:9-11), the Spirit crowns the scene, diffusing the flames of his presence.
The artist's lively creativity tempts our eye away from the central group to consider three revealing details. First, in the upper right, God's hand reaches out from the heavenly clouds to bless and impart the divine words: "You are my beloved Son." Next, at the bottom right, the figure of the serpent, the personification of evil, is vanquished by the One who "for our salvation came down from heaven." And finally, to the left, delighting in this scene, the angel—God's messenger—is busy watering the tree of knowledge which through the Savior, the new Adam, and his baptism has become the tree of Life.

divinity, consubstantial with us as regards his humanity."

In phrase after phrase, the Creed stresses the true humanity of Christ. "He was incarnate. . . and became man." This emphasis attests to the essential optimism of Christianity. Plato could say that the body is a tomb; Gnostics and others yearned to escape from it. In contrast, the Creed teaches that God himself willed to take on human flesh, and thus it affirms the essential goodness of humanity. We may have fallen by sin, but we can be raised up from sin, too; we can hope to be freed from corruption, by the Word who became flesh and dwelt among us (Jn 1:14).

All of this speculation is summed up by Saint Athanasius of Alexandria, the great opponent of Arianism, who wrote, early in the fourth century, that "He indeed assumed humanity that we might become God." The Church never tires of pondering the mystery of salvation, that God willed us to be saved by one like us in all things but sin. One of the Eucharistic prefaces in the Roman Missal sums up this mystery beautifully: "For we know it belongs to your boundless glory, that you came to the aid of mortal beings with your divinity and even fashioned for us a remedy out of mortality itself, that the cause of our downfall might become the means of our salvation." ■

Next page:
Konrad Witz (1400-1445), ***The Decision of the Redemption*** *(c. 1444), oil on wood, 62.6 x 52 in.*

For the believer, nothing is more important than the encounter with the Lord. Because God came down to us by taking on our human condition, Eternity entered time, the Invisible was made present. In order to do so, and as further proof of his humility, he had need of one of us—Mary. Witz here incorporates subtlety and his own meditation on the mystery. To the left, installed in the majesty and splendor of the heavenly throne, we behold the gathering of the Holy Trinity. The Father leafs through a book of sacred history—a story continued here with the descent of the Spirit through whose power the Son will be made incarnate. Jesus is the Lamb of God "who takes away the sins of the world." He, the true key to paradise, establishes the definitive covenant with mankind by which we are redeemed. The artist depicts the seeds of eternity, John the Baptist and Jesus, nestled in the hearts of Elizabeth and Mary. In contrasting simplicity to the scene on the left, here on the right the two women embrace, uniting their vocation which is ours as well: to welcome God into our lives. Thus, the magnificence of the rich fabrics, the gilded furnishings set with precious stones, all herald the splendor of salvation granted to each one of us.

The Lord Abandoned on the Cross

Thus trimmed forth, they bring me to the rout,
Who *Crucify him,* cry with one strong shout.
God holds His peace at man, and man cries out.
Was ever grief like mine?

They lead me in once more, and putting then
Mine own clothes on they lead me out again.
Whom devils fly, thus is He tossed of men:
Was ever grief like mine?

And now weary of sport, glad to engross
All spite in one, counting my life their loss,
They carry me to my most bitter cross:
Was ever grief like mine?

My cross I bear myself, until I faint:
Then Simon bears it for me by constraint,
The decreed burden of each mortal saint:
Was ever grief like mine?

O all ye who pass by, behold and see;
Man stole the fruit, but I must climb the tree;
The tree of life to all, but only me:
Was ever grief like mine?

Lo, here I hang, charged with a world of sin,
The greater world o' th' two; for that came in
By words, but this by sorrow I must win:
Was ever grief like mine?

Such sorrow, as if sinful man could feel,
Or feel his part, he would not cease to kneel
Till all were melted, though he were all steel:
Was ever grief like mine?

But *O my God, my God!* why leav'st Thou me,
The Son, in whom Thou dost delight to be?
My God, my God—
Never was grief like mine.

George Herbert
From "The Sacrifice"

Crucifixus etiam pro nobis

For our sake he was crucified under Pontius Pilate, he suffered death and was buried,

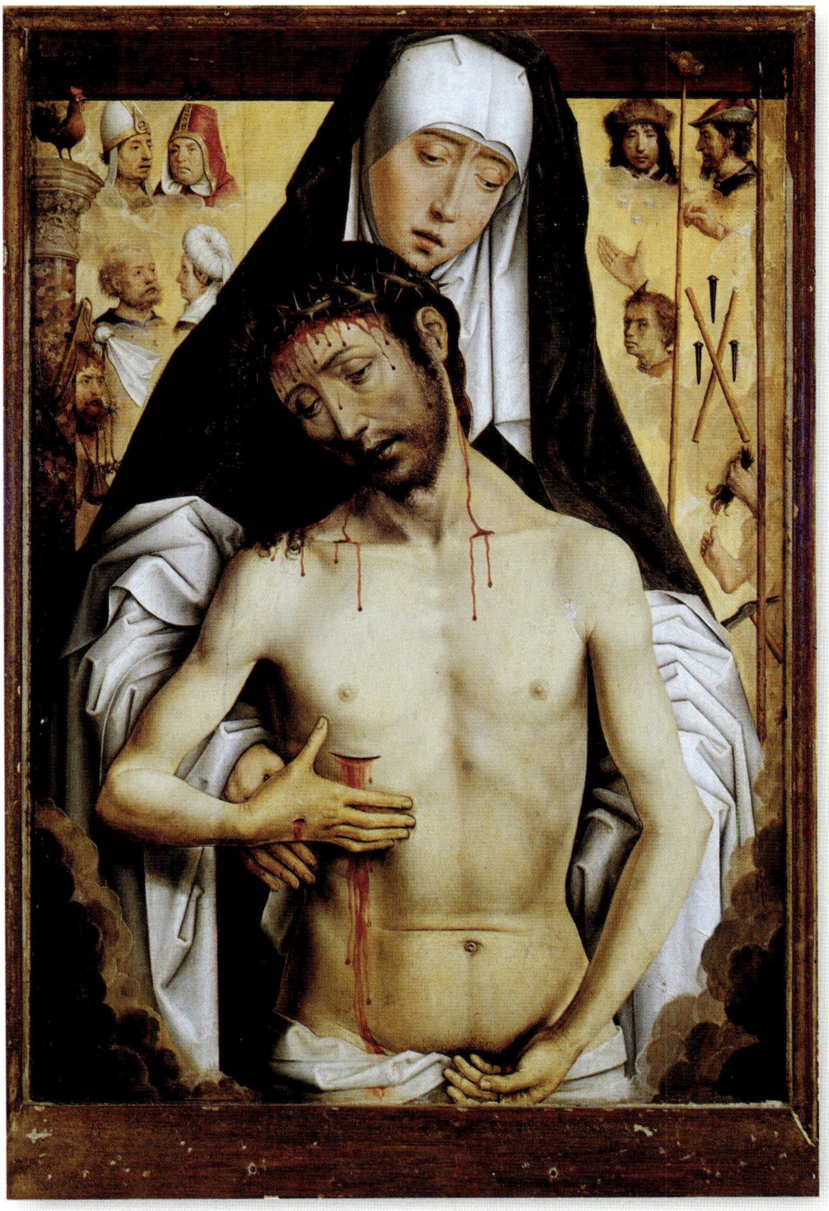

Remember your mercies, O Lord,
and with your eternal protection sanctify your servants,
for whom Christ your Son,
by the shedding of his Blood,
established the Paschal Mystery.

Previous page:
Hans Memling (c. 1430-1494), ***The Virgin Presenting the Man of Sorrows*** *(c. 1480)*
oil on wood, 20.5 x 14 in.

Mary. Stabat mater at the foot of the cross. You experienced the Passion of your son, the Son of God, within the deepest recesses of your own flesh. You could have hidden away your vast sorrow. But instead, once again, you offer it to us. Here is fulfilled the prophecy uttered by the aged Simeon at the first Presentation: "And you yourself a sword will pierce." Yes, you suffer, and two tears roll down your cheeks. Your Son is crowned with thorns. In a moving gesture of offering and infinite self-giving, he cups his open left hand below the blood flowing from his pierced side. Here too is all the violence of the Passion: the symbols, faces, gestures form the vocabulary of this composition worthy of a surrealist. These are the hands that slapped, struck, whipped, tore his hair. There is the foot that must have kicked the condemned man. The hammer, nails, whipping post, scourge, lance, and sponge soaked in vinegar are like stepping stones along the path of the Man of Sorrows. No word is spoken. We enter into this encounter with God in silence. Discreetly, perched atop a pillar to the left, the cock crows: Are we among those who betray the Savior, abandon him, cause him to suffer?

Modern science has taught us amazing things about the universe—its unimaginable size, with millions upon millions of galaxies, and its great age, measured in billions of years. Yet no matter how enormous the universe is, we know where its center is. No matter how many billions of years it has existed and will perdure, we know the fulcrum of its history. The center of all space and time is a small hill outside the city of Jerusalem, on a dark Friday afternoon.

Three men hang on crosses, condemned to die, slowly and brutally, for their crimes. Two were common criminals; one was condemned for a different crime. Over his head hung a sign: "Jesus of Nazareth, King of the Jews." Pontius Pilate had written it. The man who sneered, "What is truth?" wrote the truest of all statements.

Perhaps the most surprising word in the Creed is "Pontius Pilate." After all, the Creed is a profession of Christian faith; yet, at its very heart, we name a third-rate Roman administrator who was eventually removed from office for mismanagement. Pontius Pilate was the prefect of the Roman province of Judea from AD 26 to 36. But the fact that Pontius Pilate is a historical figure serves a crucial purpose in the Creed: to say that Jesus was crucified "under Pontius Pilate" is the opposite of saying that he suffered "once upon

Tintoretto (1518-1594), ***Christ before Pilate*** *(1566-1567)*
oil on canvas, 203 x 149 in., Venice, Scuola Grande di San Rocco

We are here at the end of the dialogue between Jesus and the Roman procurator as recorded in the Gospels. Having come to a verdict—written down by the scribe seated below the judge's bench—Pilate washes his hands. As he does so, he turns toward one of the accusers wearing a turban, saying, "I am innocent of this man's blood. Look to it yourselves" (Mt 27:24). The harsh light enveloping Jesus underscores the contrast between his calm self-possession and the agitation of the crowd. His very silence sets him apart. Their clothing and faces identify the onlookers as contemporaries of Tintoretto; the outfit of the high priest testifies that the Orient was in vogue. Jesus alone is timeless, eternal. Venice provides the backdrop for the scene: architectural elements suggest the majestic and lofty palace of the Serenissima, reinforcing the impression that for the artist, as for ourselves, the condemnation of the just One remains an ever topical event.

a time." Once upon a time is the time of fairy tales; "under Pontius Pilate" is real, historical time. Our redemption is not part of some cosmic myth; it is a historical fact.

The Creed affirms that Jesus truly suffered death, and that his body was buried. Every detail of what happened in those hours, late on a Friday afternoon, has been the subject of meditation and prayer, and motifs for painters and sculptors. Perhaps the most famous theme in art drawn from these events is the Pietà, the depiction of Mary holding the corpse of Jesus in her arms.

Agnolo di Cosimo, known as Bronzino (1503-1572), ***The Crucifixion*** *(c. 1540)*
oil on canvas, 57 x 45.3 in.

Despite his extreme pallor, he's not quite dead yet. What's more, the lance has not yet pierced his side. Alone, abandoned by all, the crucified Jesus is not depicted in the usual landscape. The cross of precious wood leans against the pilasters of an apse in a sixteenth-century church. The crucifix Bronzino presents here is a veritable sculpture in trompe-l'oeil. Its striking realism offers for contemplation a man in his death throes before our very eyes. This then is Jesus crucified who, as the Eucharistic sacrifice on the altar of every church, gives his life, his Body and his Blood, to those who come to receive it. Here, there is no cry, no groaning—just this magnificent body which, of course, corresponds to the canons of beauty of Renaissance art but, more importantly, is an evocation of the gift of love and of life.

But devotion has pondered many other details, too.

Once he was assured that Jesus was dead, Pilate released his body to his family and friends. The body would have been taken down from the cross, as the nails were removed; and perhaps the nails were laid aside. The body would have been washed and wrapped in a shroud. The Evangelists tell us

Jean-Michel Alberola, ***The Sacred Heart*** *(1989)*
oil on paper, 39.4 x 25.2 in.

Red. Blood. Black. Death.
Jesus is crucified. A mere brushstroke or two underscore his presence on the cross but are enough to evoke the more vivid crucifixes seared in our memory. Alberola outlines the silhouette nailed to the instrument of torture. The superimposed face of the One whom the prophet Isaiah referred to as the Suffering Servant is barely visible, hidden beneath the flat black patch of paint. It is a darkness which allows us to imagine the face of all those who, oppressed, humiliated, abused, are one with Jesus, those who like him are crucified. But it would be wrong to think that the Church celebrates any exaltation of suffering in contemplating Christ crucified. In the midst of the bloody and deadly maelstrom, a ray of hope shines out in the darkness. The wound in Christ's side, from which blood and water pour forth, is luminous, as is the white loincloth which calls to mind his shroud. This slashed side is an opening to the Resurrection. The blood and water spilled out of love is the tidal flow that bears us into eternal life.

Jacopo Pontormo (1494-1557), ***The Deposition*** *(1526)*
oil on wood, 123 x 75.5 in., Florence, Church of Santa Felicità

If you ever have the privilege to visit Florence, make sure to enter the doors of the little church of Saint Felicity, right near the Ponte Vecchio. Immediately to the right on entering, I guarantee you a thrill of emotion as you come face to face with this magisterial work by Pontormo, whose self-portrait appears discreetly on the right in the role of Nicodemus. Admire these complicated figures and their affected poses—surprising to behold in this tragic scene. Mary, collapsing, draws the attention of three women. Observe the faces of the two young men carrying the body of Jesus: the alarm on the angelic face on the left; the silent and sad appeal of the one kneeling. This body is the Panis Angelicus *given for us at every celebration of the Eucharist on the altar above which this painting hangs, the altar on which this languid body of Christ might be laid. What subtlety in the gesture of the woman veiled in pink who leans down tenderly to support the head of the Savior. Give in to the astonishing effect of these unreal, acid colors, devoid of all shadow, and further intensified by a deep, warm glow that lends this masterpiece a dazzling and evocative dimension.*

Next page:
The Master of Chaource, ***The Entombment*** *(1515)*
polychromed stone, 75 x 121 x 56 in., Chaource, France, Church of Saint John the Baptist

They are all present, faithful to the One they loved and followed. Just as we do for a loved one, those close to Jesus attend to his burial. "The noble Joseph, taking down thine immaculate body from the Tree, wrapped it in clean linen with spices, and mourning, placed it in a new tomb." This verse from the Divine Liturgy of Saint Basil the Great poignantly ushers us into the scene. On either side of the group, Joseph of Arimathea and Nicodemus lay down the body of Christ. Mary inclines her head over his face. Behind her stands the beloved disciple John in contemplation. The holy women bear the symbols of the Passion, while Mary Magdalene holds the already opened jar of myrrh and aloes—the aromatic spices used according to Jewish custom for the burial of the dead. The execution as well as the restrained and contemplative expressions are reminiscent of the art of northern Europe and allows space for a ninth participant in the scene: the viewer yourself!

that Joseph of Arimathea oversaw the rite of burial (see Mt 27:57–60 and parallels). Saint John adds a further detail: Nicodemus, who had come to Jesus by night, joined in the burial ritual and contributed about one hundred pounds of myrrh and aloes, which were spread over Jesus's body inside the linen shroud (Jn 19:39–40). Saint John also tells us that Jesus was buried in a garden near Calvary, in a new tomb, in which no one had ever been buried. And finally, the tomb was sealed with a great stone.

The details of Jesus' burial give us much to ponder. The dominant motif is that of a Jewish funeral. The body is washed and wrapped in a shroud. The burial takes place quickly, because the sabbath began at sunset, and the sabbath that year fell during Passover.

But other details suggest that this was not an ordinary burial. Besides the large quantity of myrrh and aloes, Jesus, burial in a new tomb stands out. In a subtle way, the phrase suggests that Jesus is not being buried among the other dead; his burial is somehow exceptional. And the word "new" adds another note: "new" is one of the most important words used to describe Easter. Even the gloom and apparent despair of Good Friday already have a glimmer of Easter hope.

What does faith teach us? Just as Jesus was true man, so too he truly died. The Son of God died on the cross, for us men and for our salvation. We pray, "We adore thee, O Christ, and we bless thee, because by thy holy cross thou hast redeemed the world."

The cross of Christ, once a sign of shame and disgrace, has become the central symbol of Christian faith, and of its glory. Our churches are marked by a cross on their roofs or steeples. Our houses ought to have a crucifix displayed where everyone can see it. We begin our prayers, and the Mass, with the sign of the cross. The Christian cross is to be seen in countless places. Sometimes it is made of two plain pieces of wood; sometimes it is made of gold and encrusted with jewels. But the message is always the same: the heart of our faith, the heart of our Redemption, is the mystery of Christ's cross, the symbol of triumph over sin and death, and of life without end. ■

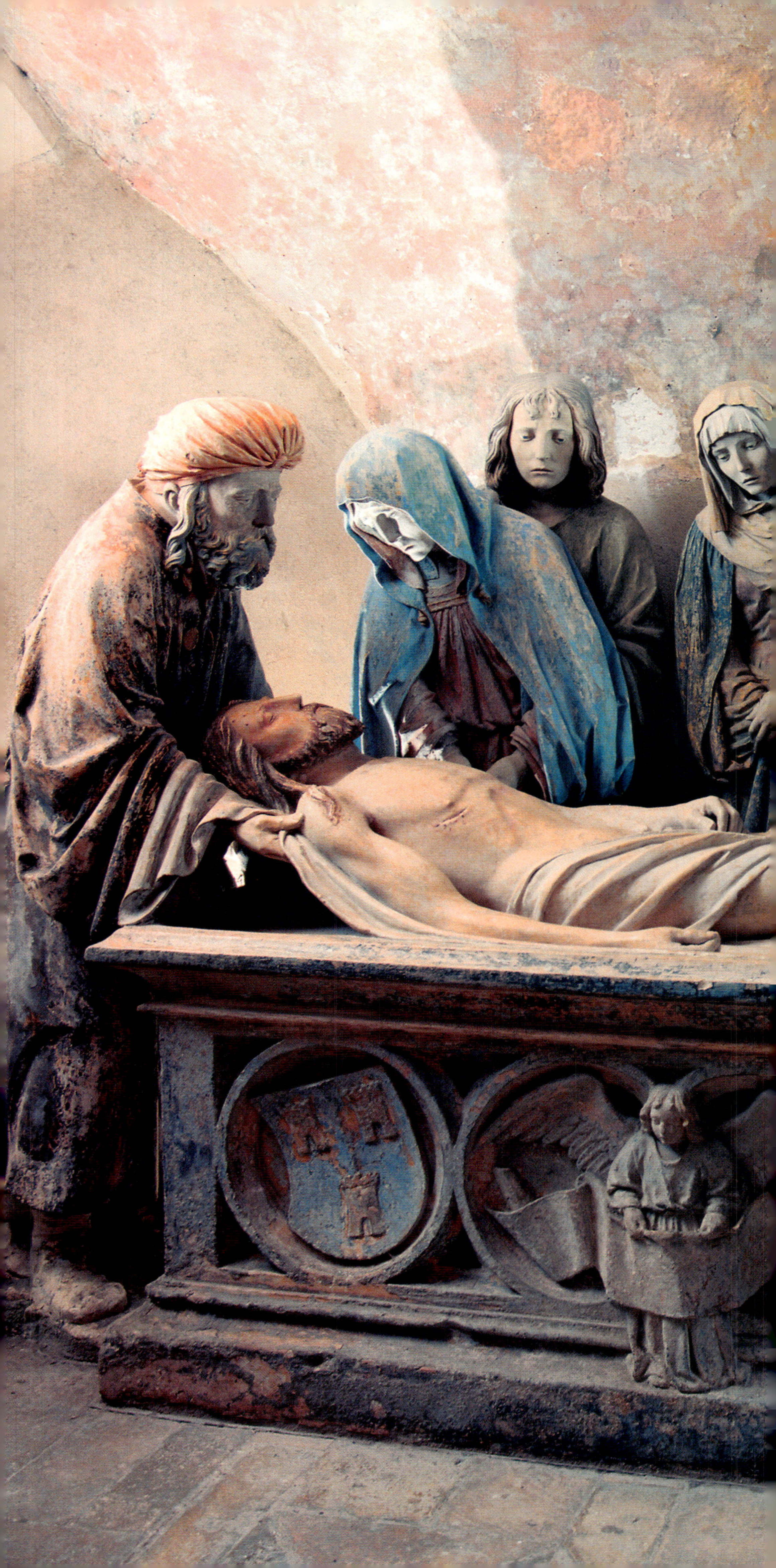

The True and Only Day

I got me flowers to strew Thy way,
I got me boughs off many a tree,
But Thou wast up by break of day
And brought'st Thy sweets along with Thee.

The sun arising in the east,
Thou he give light, and the east, perfume,
If they should offer to contest
With Thy arising, they presume.

Can there be any day but this,
Thou many suns to shine endeavor?
We count three hundred, but we miss:
There is but one, and that one ever.

George Herbert
From "Easter"

Et resurrexit tertia die

and rose again on the third day
in accordance with the Scriptures.

The Pascha beautiful,
The Pascha of the Lord,
The Pascha,
The Pascha all honorable has dawned for us.
The Pascha!
On which let us embrace one another with joy.
O Pascha! A ransom for sorrow.
For today shining forth from the tomb
As from the bridal chamber
Christ filled the women with joy saying,
"Proclaim the glad tidings to the Apostles."

What does "he rose" mean? As the four Gospels describe it, Jesus came back to life in his human body. He appeared to his disciples. They touched him, touched his wounds. They conversed with him. He ate and drank in their presence. But the life he returned to was not the life he had experienced before his crucifixion. He returned to a higher, more exalted form of life.

Jesus Christ rose "in accordance with the Scriptures." This phrase in the Creed is drawn from Saint Paul: "I delivered to you as of first importance what I also received, that Christ died for our sins in accordance with the scriptures, that he was buried, that he was raised on the third day in accordance with the scriptures . . ." (1 Cor 15:3–4). To affirm that Jesus Christ rose from the dead "in accordance with the Scriptures" is to affirm the continuity of the Old Testament with the New. In the second century, a heretic named Marcion wanted to banish the Old Testament from the Church's canon of inspired books. He had read the Scriptures and thought that he discovered two Gods: the God of justice of the Old Testament, the creator and lawgiver, and the God of love of the New Testament, a greater and higher God, the Father of our Lord Jesus Christ. By rejecting Marcion, the Church affirmed some key truths. There is one God, and one God only. The one God, who is the Father of Jesus Christ, truly created the world. He truly called Abraham out of Ur of the Chaldees; he truly spoke to Moses from the burning bush; he truly gave the law on Sinai; he truly spoke through the prophets.

The account of the first Passover in the Book of Exodus helps us understand Christ's Paschal Mystery. There "passover" has two meanings. Exodus chapter 12 narrates how God ordered the Israelites in Egypt to kill a lamb and smear its blood on their doorposts. God slaughtered the firstborn of the Egyptians that night, but he "passed over" the houses smeared with blood. Thus, passover was an act of divine grace. That same night, Pharaoh released the Israelites from servitude, and they left Egypt. When they got to the

Previous page:
The Holy Women at the Tomb *(late 18th-early 19th century)*
stained glass, detail, north rose window, diameter 21.2 in., Cathedral of Sées, France

On the morning of the first day of the week, three women go to the tomb bearing spices to embalm the body of Jesus. We catch them here just as they discover the tomb is empty. Admire their varied poses. One, on the left, carrying a jar of aromatic spices, is suprised. The second, her arms outstretched, turns her head with a puzzled look toward the empty stone tomb in total bewilderment. The third, with a gesture of amazement, her eyes wide with wonder, is already reaching out her upraised palms in a gesture of praise and thanksgiving. The colors, kindled by the enlivening light, heighten the story as depicted in this expressive image: green, the sign of hope; the blue of eternity; the red flame of divine love—all set my faith on fire, impelling me to proclaim: Christ is risen!

Page 54:
Domínikos Theotokópoulos, known as El Greco (1541-1614), ***The Resurrection*** *(1597-1600) oil on canvas, 108 x 50 in.*

At the heart of faith—the Resurrection. Let joy burst forth: "The hosts of heaven, exult, let the angel ministers of God exult!" Let us make this Easter prayer of rejoicing our own as we enter into this quivering image to experience the surging flood of eternal life. The tomb has disappeared; it is no longer of importance. We take part in this encounter between dazzled, stunned humanity and this man-God gradually drifting away. He floats in the air, serene and glowing, his glorious body as bright as the banner of victory in his supple hand: it bears a strong resemblance to his shroud, until this moment a symbol of shadows and death. The brilliance of his halo sets off the glittering red of his swirling cloak. We recall that it was "necessary that the Messiah should suffer these things and enter into his glory" (Lk 24:26). What do we feel amid this throng of sleeping, suprised, blinded soldiers as we hear them falling to the ground? Jesus has conquered death, symbolized by their weapons. They were supposed to guard the tomb to avoid any trouble but they are powerless in the face of this supernatural outburst, this unforeseen upheaval. Do you observe the hand of the soldier in the blue tunic, bewildered by this ascending figure? This massive figure of humanity, now redeemed, cannot grasp the risen One, who appears to be escaping. But Christ responds with an almost identical gesture of invitation: Come follow me on this path to glory!

Red Sea, God dried it up, and the people "passed over" the sea dryshod. Thus, passover was also an experience of liberation, from slavery to freedom. Both passovers are fulfilled in Christ. The blood of the Lamb of God, shed on the cross, saves his people from the death of sin, and the Christian people pass through the waters of baptism into freedom.

For all that the Scriptures have to say about Jesus' Resurrection, they are silent about the event itself. That moment was the moment of the most intimate and intense relationship between God and Jesus. Two days before, Jesus had cried out on the cross, "My God, my God, why have you forsaken me?" (Mt 27:46; Ps 22:1). He died, and his body was laid in the tomb. Then, sometime as morning approached on the day after the sabbath, that dead body came alive. But more than alive—alive with a higher and greater kind of life than we can yet imagine. The heart beat, the blood flowed, the eyes opened. In a blinding flash, Jesus knew and understood. He was Messiah and Lord; he was the Lord of History. In that

William Bouguereau (1825-1905), ***The Holy Women at the Tomb*** *(1890) oil on canvas, 63.2 x 102 in.*

The genius unique to every artist enables us to experience what we cannot ourselves express. Here we find Mary Magdalene, Mary of Clopas, and Salome before the tomb of Jesus. Thanks to his almost photographic technique and archeological detail, the artist plunges us back into the time of Jesus: we are present at the announcement of the Resurrection by this youthful luminous being, this heavenly messenger— "He is not here. . ." The majestic figures of the women, draped in mourning garments, cluster together at the entrance to the funeral chamber in an artistically posed group. They can now dry the discreet tears that mar their elegant faces. Bouguereau's highly meticulous, indeed, impeccable style invites us to linger over a few details. Observe the rendering of the delicate hands grasping the upright of the door or the round stone, or those firmly clasped together. Above all, notice the splash of reflected light on the face of the kneeling woman: it is an echo of this Life which henceforth glows within every person of faith.

Rembrandt (1606-1669)
Christ and the Two Disciples on the Road to Emmaus *(c. 1655)*
ink, bistre, and wash, 6.5 x 8.8 in.

This most common of journeys will end in the greatest of revelations, with the most thrilling of announcements: the Good News! At the edge of a humble Middle Eastern village—the horseman's outfit in the background confirms the location—three men converse. Each represents a period of life: youth, adulthood, old age. The eldest, with an austere expression, seems engrossed in grave and detailed explanations. The youngest listens, crestfallen. We recognize them, these disciples of Jesus who set out on the road after the tragedy of the Passion. As their outfits and attributes imply, they are once again pilgrims. Like us, they are traveling through this vale of tears that is life. But, like us, they are joined by the risen One who, for those "set on pilgrim roads," makes of it an oasis "of spring water" (see Ps 84:6, 7). And like us, too often, they do not recognize him. Not yet—even though he explains to them how all has happened "in accordance with the Scriptures." Yes, we too must truly come to know the Son of God before we can recognize him. Through these rough and rapid strokes of Rembrandt's pen, we realize that it is in the simplicity of everyday life, within the human heart, that Jesus comes to meet us and reveal himself as the living One, walking by our side for eternity.

Next page:
Fra Angelico (c. 1400-1455), **Noli Me Tangere** *(1440-1442)*
fresco, 65.3 x 49.2 in., Florence, Convent of San Marco

With joy we once again immerse ourselves in the serene atmosphere created by this blessed artist in one of the cells of the Dominican convent in Florence where many a religious once meditated. Let us follow their lead and enter into one of the most beautiful encounters ever. We are in the lush flowering garden of the Song of Songs. Nature, in the springtime of rebirth, accompanies the risen One who, standing before his tomb, is called by Mary Magdelene. She mistakes him for the gardener, an error given visual form by the hoe Jesus carries. She asks for the body which she believes has been taken away. Fra Angelico gives us a snapshot of this very moment: "Mary!"—her name cuts through the silence of this morning of renewal. Suddenly she grasps that only one person in the world could call her with such compassion and love. "Rabboni!"—instant recognition. In an understandable rush of emotion, she reaches out her arms to embrace him. But Christ stops her: "Do not hold onto me." What must she feel? What joy! The power of life and love itself manifest before her! Mary Magdalene thus becomes the first to announce the Good News: "I have seen the Lord" (Jn 20:18).

moment, Jesus the Christ was united with God his Father in such an intense act of love that the risen body of Christ was joined for ever to the Blessed Trinity.

The risen Christ is first of all the consoler. In his *Spiritual Exercises*, Saint Ignatius Loyola asks us to meditate on an event that is not mentioned in the Scriptures, but which he is certain happened. The Scriptures tell us that Jesus appeared to his disciples, and to Mary Magdalene and the women. But the first person he appeared to, Saint Ignatius assures us, was his own mother. Perhaps she was less surprised than anyone else. Redemption had begun because she had said, in perfect faith, "Let it be done to me according to your word" (Lk 1:38). The loving mother, who had stood at the foot of the cross and watched her only Son die, now sees him standing alive before her. Have a mother and a son ever loved each other more? ■

Drawing Us Up into Victory

Sing we triumphant hymns of praise,
New hymns to heaven exulting raise:
Christ, by a road before untrod,
Ascendeth to the throne of God.

Thy holy apostolic band
Upon the Mount of Olives stand,
And with the Virgin Mother see
Jesus' resplendent majesty.

To whom the Angels, drawing nigh,
"Why stand and gaze upon the sky?
This is the Savior!" thus they say,
"This is His noble triumph day!"

"Again ye shall behold Him, so
As ye today have seen Him go;
In glorious pomp ascending high,
Up to the portals of the sky."

O grant us thitherward to tend,
And with unwearied hearts ascend,
Toward Thy kingdom's throne, where Thou,
As is our faith, art seated now.

Be Thou our joy and strong defense,
Who art our future recompense:
So shall the light that springs from Thee
Be ours through all eternity.

O risen Christ, ascended Lord,
All praise to Thee let earth accord,
Who art, while endless ages run,
With Father and with Spirit One.

The Venerable Bede
From *Hymnum canamus gloriae*

Et ascendit in caelum

He ascended into heaven
and is seated at the right hand of the Father.

*He who came down is he who has now risen higher
than all the heavens. Alleluia.*

*O gates, lift high your heads;
grow higher, ancient doors.
Let him enter, the king of glory!*

*Who is he, the king of glory?
He, the Lord of armies,
he is the king of glory.*

Previous page:
The Ascension *(15th century)*
ivory, 3.9 x 1.8 in.

He is no longer here. Only his feet and the hem of his tunic remain visible. With the Apostles, we watch as Jesus rises up. He who had condescended to embrace us, even unto the cross, now "is seated at the right hand of the Father." In this panel from an ivory casket, the Apostles stare up at the sky, perhaps with regret. They resemble little children kneeling as they say their prayers, with hands joined in worship. In the center, the deserted hilltop draws the eye—an emptiness in itself indicative of the difficulty of expressing the physical presence of Jesus. He is going away, but not abandoning us. The Ascension of the Lord calls us to strive to follow "in the Savior's footsteps, to the place where for our sake he entered before us" (Ascension Prayer after Communion). Jesus, taken up to heaven, carries us along in his wake, calling us to share in his glorified life. "Let us hold unwaveringly to our confession that gives us hope, for he who made the promise is trustworthy" (Heb 10:23).

The Acts of the Apostles provides the fullest account of our Lord's Ascension into heaven: "As they were looking on, he was lifted up, and a cloud took him out of their sight. And while they were gazing into heaven as he went, behold two men stood by them in white robes, and said, 'Men of Galilee, why do you stand looking into heaven? This Jesus, who was taken up from you into heaven, will come in the same way as you saw him go into heaven'" (Acts 1:9–11). Forty days after the first Easter, Jesus took leave of his disciples, and the Resurrection appearances ceased. But the narrative does not end there. The image of the disciples standing on the Mount of Olives, looking up, mouths agape, is an amusing one. The two angels rebuke them gently, asking why they are dwelling on the past. Christ's mission has been accomplished. In ten days, the era of the Church will begin. And at the end of time, Christ will return.

Saint John, in his Gospel, gives us a different insight into the Ascension. On Easter morning, Mary Magdalene is weeping at Jesus's tomb. Jesus comes to her and says, "Mary." John continues: "Jesus said to her, 'Do not hold me, for I have not yet ascended to the Father; but go to my brethren and say to them, I am ascending to my Father and your Father, to my God and your God'" (Jn 20:17). The Ascension is an essential part of God's plan of salvation, which is not complete until Christ ascends into heaven.

In the older liturgy, the paschal candle was extinguished after the reading of the Gospel on Ascension Thursday, suggesting somehow that a light had gone out. There was a twinge of sadness in that moment, although the sadness was not grounded in solid Christian doctrine. The Ascension does not mean that Christ is absent, but that he is present in a new way. That way, of course, is in the Holy Spirit. In the beautiful Last Discourse in Saint John's Gospel, Jesus says to the disciples, "It is to your advantage that I go away, for if I do not go away, the Counselor will not come to you; but if I go, I will send him to you" (Jn 16:7).

The article of the Creed about the incarnate Christ calls us to ponder his life in the past, in the present, and in the future. The final past event that the Creed

Andrea della Robbia (1435-1525), ***The Ascension of Christ*** *(1490)*
terra cotta, 180 x 121 in., La Verna, Chiesa Maggiore

Heaven and earth. Lush green nature and azure skies. And the diaphanous figures of a universe experiencing separation and fullness of communion at the same time. "Men of Galilee, why are you standing there looking up at the sky? This Jesus who has been taken up from you into heaven will return in the same way as you have seen him going into heaven" (Acts 1:11). Once again, the heavenly host, represented by angels and the frieze of cherubim, participate in this biblical event. I am no angel, yet my eye too is drawn toward the group of kneeling Apostles. I too am a disciple of the Lord and cannot help but raise my eyes in contemplation of him. Just moments ago, Mary and the disciples were standing right next to him. Like them, I believe in these mysterious words of the angels inviting me not to just stand and stare but to live my life here and now in the promise of eternity, henceforth accompanied by Jesus. Our paschal joy goes on, as the garland of leaves and fruit suggests—a signature trait of this Florentine family studio whose work will ever be identified with Tuscany.

Pieter de Grebber (c. 1600-c. 1652),
***God Invites Christ to Be Seated on the Throne at His Right Hand** (1645)*
oil on canvas, 46,6 x 53.5 in.

Art can sometimes upset, disturb, or unnerve. Perhaps this painting may have that effect on you. Or at least provoke a bit of surprise. Let us take a step back to try to understand the artist's motivation. How can the relationship between the persons of the Trinity be represented other than by almost unavoidably reducing it to what we can understand within our own limited human hearts. Let us dare to suggest this as the "return" of the Son following his Ascension. Various instruments of betrayal and torment are spread at the foot of the heavenly throne. Jesus kneels on the cross, clothed in the mantle of the Passion and still wearing the crown of thorns. But he is risen: he displays the wounds in his hands. Thus reunited within the communion of the Trinity, bathed in the bright rays of the Spirit, he presents himself before his Father. God is a figure of majestic, omnipotent, imperial—and here—even papal power, since he wears a tiara, the symbol of his authority. It is true, such a reductive expression of divinity is perhaps inappropriate and limited, focusing as it does solely on the concept of power. We cannot find that wholly satisfying. Yet, undoubtedly unique in Western art, here is this gesture of welcome and the invitation to be seated at the right hand of the Creator. We certainly cannot speak of warmth or great emotion here. Nevertheless, the subject is the promise of salvation to, and gratitude of, all those who profess that Christ shares in his Father's glory. Thus, we are to know and remain in him, though perhaps not in such a staid and strait-laced spirit! But that too is part of the confrontation, through art, between different generations.

records is Christ's Ascension into heaven. The Creed describes his present existence, from the Ascension to the Second Coming, as his being seated at the right hand of the Father. In biblical language, to sit at the ruler's right hand is to be his viceroy, second in command. (Two of Jesus's disciples once asked to sit as his right hand and at his left; see Mk 10:37). In the next clause, the Creed will speak of Jesus Christ's second coming.

In his present existence, Christ is High Priest, leading his Church in the one perfect act of worship of the Father. In words attributed to Saint Augustine, "Christ prays for us, he prays in us, he is prayed to by us" (sermon on Saint Stephen). After the Ascension, Christ hears our prayers; he prays to the Father for us; and, since we are his Body, he prays in us. He is also present to us in the Eucharist. Each day, the Holy

Sacrifice of the Mass is offered on countless altars throughout the world, and, thereby, the one perfect sacrifice of Calvary is made present and effective for us, and Christ the Lord is offered to us in Holy Communion. ■

Next page:
Triptych of the Trinity *(16th century)*
paint on gilded wood, 11.8 x 17.7 in.

There is almost a family resemblance here in the central panel of this triptych. Seated side by side on the same throne, the eternal God and Christ his Son jointly present the Book of Life opened to reveal the divine nature of Jesus: "I am the way and the truth and the life" (Jn 14:6). They both raise their right hand, the Father in blessing and the Son to display the nail wounds, clearly visible along with the other marks of the crucifixion. Their shared golden cloak is lined with colors distinguishing their two identities: red, recalling the Passion, and the blue of divine eternity. Behind them, through an opening reminiscent of a Gothic stained-glass window, the starry sky locates them in caelum, *as evoked in the Creed.*

VIA

ERITAS
T
ITA

He Is Near, Even at the Gates

At the name of Jesus
Every knee shall bow,
Every tongue confess Him
King of glory now;
'Tis the Father's pleasure
We should call Him Lord,
Who from the beginning
Was the mighty Word.

At His voice creation
Sprang at once to sight,
All the angel faces,
All the hosts of light,
Thrones and dominations,
Stars upon their way,
All the heavenly orders
In their great array.

Humbled for a season,
To receive a name
From the lips of sinners
Unto whom He came,
Faithfully He bore it
Spotless to the last,
Brought it back victorious
When from death He passed.

Bore it up triumphant
With its human light,
Through all ranks of creatures,
To the central height,
To the throne of Godhead,
To the Father's breast;
Filled it with the glory
Of that perfect rest.

Name Him, brothers, name Him,
With love strong as death,
But with awe and wonder,
And with bated breath;
He is God the Savior,
He is Christ the Lord,
Ever to be worshipped,
Trusted, and adored.

In your hearts enthrone Him;
There let Him subdue
All that is not holy,
All that is not true;
Crown Him as your captain
In temptation's hour;
Let His will enfold you
In its light and power.

Brothers, this Lord Jesus
Shall return again,
With His Father's glory,
With His angel train;
For all wreaths of empire
Meet upon His brow,
And our hearts confess Him
King of glory now.

Caroline M. Noel
From "At the Name of Jesus"

Et iterum venturus est cum gloria

He will come again in glory
to judge the living and the dead
and his kingdom will have no end.

For he assumed at his first coming
the lowliness of human flesh,
and so fulfilled the design you formed long ago,
and opened for us the way to eternal salvation,
that, when he comes again in glory and majesty
and all is at last made manifest,
we who watch for that day
may inherit the great promise
in which now we dare to hope.

Previous page:
The Last Judgment *(13th century)*
illumination, 11.8 x 7.9 in.

Christ comes again in glory. Seated with the clouds as his footstool, he shows his wounds. At his sides, angels hold the instruments of the Passion. "All the tribes of the earth. . .will see the Son of Man coming upon the clouds of heaven. . .And he will send out his angels with a trumpet blast, and they will gather his elect from the four winds, from one end of the heavens to the other" (Mt 24:30-31). No one knows the day nor the hour. For this reason, the atemporality of the event is suggested by a golden background against which the figures of the dead are depicted awakening at the sound of the angels' trumpet blast. The interplay of their gazes draws us into a heavenly progression. In the lower register, the angels turn toward those they are calling. And they—one full of gratitude, raising his arms in prayerful praise; others in surprise and expectation—turn toward their Redeemer and Judge. But Christ looks straight at us. He alone calls to us, drawing us to himself through his direct and piercing gaze.

Christians can be the most confident people in the world. Compare them with optimists. Optimists affirm that things are going to get better, that it will all turn out well. But they simply affirm; they do not know. Christians have no need for optimism; they have hope. And hope is assurance. We know, as the Creed teaches, how the Great Story is going to end: it will end with the return of Christ in glory, to reign as King of the universe. The Church celebrates the Solemnity of Christ the King on the last Sunday of the year, and the preface of the Mass for that feast describes Christ's kingdom in memorable words: "an eternal and universal kingdom, a kingdom of truth and life, a kingdom of holiness and grace, a kingdom of justice, love, and peace."

The Creed also teaches us, however, a more sober truth. Christ will return as judge. He will pass judgment on "the living and the dead," every human being. The judgment reminds us that the way we live, whether our lives are characterized by good or evil, will make a difference—an eternal difference. Catholic theologians write of the Four Last Things: death, judgment, heaven, and hell; and it does no good to ignore them, or to pretend that they are only mythic.

"And his kingdom will have no end." This phrase is a curious one, unless we know its background. One of the earliest, but not the most profound, opponents of Arianism was a bishop named Marcellus of Ancyra. Marcellus wrote a book in refutation of one of the sympathizers of Arius and, in an effort to defend the full and true divinity of Christ, may have speculated on an expanding and contracting Godhead. Whether he actually asserted this teaching is irrelevant. His opponents said he did, and Marcellus is remembered in history for saying that, at the end of time, Christ's kingdom would come to an end. He based his speculation on a difficult verse from Saint Paul's first letter to the Corinthians: "Then comes the end, when he delivers the kingdom to God the Father after destroying every rule and every authority and power" (1 Cor 15:24). The clause "and his kingdom will

William Blake (1757-1827), ***Christ Accepting the Office of Redeemer*** *(1808)*
Illustration to Milton's "Paradise Lost", pen and watercolor, 19.5 x 15.5 in.

Four swirling angels accompany the Redeemer. They present the crown of glory as they bow in adoration—or, rather, as they literally dive to his feet, their bodies forming a nimbus worthy of the Son of God. He who is the redemption of the human race—which Blake makes explicitly clear in the illustration's title drawn from Milton's Paradise Lost*—is received in the bosom of the Father who embraces him tenderly, without however revealing his face which we cannot know until we join him in heavenly glory. At the very bottom of the image lies Satan. With wings unfurled, he thinks to have triumphed over Adam and Eve. But, despite his weapons, he is here overcome, vanquished. Given the avant-garde choreography of these diaphanous, undulating bodies, how surprising that this work dates as early as 1808! We seem to hear dulcet harmonies beating in time with the pulse of these bodies and the folds of their robes—all bathed in suffused, ethereal light. We are indebted to this artist who, through this seemingly perpetual motion, has interpreted the spiritual dynamism that will usher us into the glory of the Father and the Son, through the Spirit, in a kingdom that will have no end.*

M CETVS STAT XPISTO IVDICE LET
CARITAS
VMILITAS
IAV CTIS GLORIA PAX REQVIE
MILI SIC STANT GAVDENTES SECVI
TIS NISI MORES IVDICIVM DVR

ERPET WSPI:DIES + PENIS INIVSTI

ILME TVENTES + FVRES O

VOBIS SSCITOTE FVTVRV

Previous page:
The Last Judgment *(detail, 1125-1135)*
tympanum, 264 x 142 in., Conques, Abbey of Sainte-Foy

The unaffected simplicity with which these twelfth-century artists interpreted the coming of Christ as judge goes right to the heart of the matter. He will come again in glory, symbolized by the mandorla on a star-studded, azure-blue background set amid the clouds. Gesturing with each hand, a majestic Jesus confirms the two pathways he unceasingly preached about: his raised right hand indicates the salvation granted the elect; his lowered left arm, the banishment of those who wandered away from God. This basic principle is reflected beneath Christ's feet in the expressions of the souls standing between Saint Michael, who welcomes the blessed, and Satan, who impatiently awaits the lost ones he covets. Behind Saint Michael lies the kingdom of bliss with the touching image of souls nestling in the bosom of Abraham. But an entirely different atmosphere reigns beyond the gates of hell where monstrous jaws swallow those about to undergo a thousand torments.

have no end" was inserted into the Creed precisely to refute Marcellus, or what people thought Marcellus had said. The fathers at Constantinople drew the phrase from the angel Gabriel's words to Mary at the Annunciation: "And he will reign over the house of Jacob for ever; and of his kingdom there will be no end" (Lk 1:33).

For us to reflect on a king and a kingdom may seem somehow foreign. The age of absolute monarchs is over. The kings and queens who still reign in some countries, mostly in Europe, are figureheads in constitutional democracies. Yet there is something romantic about a king, a charismatic person who calls his subjects to follow him. In his *Spiritual Exercises*, Saint Ignatius prepares the exercitant to meditate on the call of Christ the King by asking him to meditate on the call of an earthly king. If a good soldier would willingly follow his king into battle, how much more should we be willing to follow Christ the King! In Christ we have a king we can follow without a moment's doubt or hesitation, and the Creed assures us, "his kingdom will have no end." ■

Giotto di Bondone (c. 1266-1337), ***Christ Pantocrator*** *(1304-1306)*
fresco, Scrovegni Chapel, Padua, Italy

The Creed leads us to proclaim the goodness of the Lord throughout salvation history. The moment we affirm the perfection of Jesus' divine Sonship, we find ourselves once again in the intimacy of a personal encounter. We enter into the heavenly glory of the Savior and contemplate him who appears in majesty. The ring of light and fire surrounding him, warming us like the blaze of his love, is reflected in the cruciform halo around his head. The Book of Life gripped in his left hand offers us the hope, according to Revelation, that all the names of the faithful are inscribed within it. With his right hand, two upraised fingers signal his double nature, both human and divine, as well as his participation in the Holy Trinity (the three joined fingers). It takes the art of a Giotto, and his immediate yet meditative brushwork, to draw us into this magnificent constellation, to make of our sincere belief a new star in the firmament of faith. For it is through our faithfulness to him who died and is risen that we shall be saved.

The Breath of New Life

Our blest Redeemer, ere He breathed
His tender last farewell,
A Guide, a Comforter, bequeathed
With us to dwell.

He came in tongues of living flame,
To teach, convince, subdue;
All-powerful as the wind He came,
As viewless too.

He came sweet influence to impart,
A gracious, willing Guest,
While He can find one humble heart
Wherein to rest.

And His that gentle voice we hear,
Soft as the breath of even,
That checks each fault, that calms each fear,
And speaks of heaven.

And every virtue we possess,
And every victory won,
And every thought of holiness
Are His alone.

Spirit of purity and grace,
Our weakness, pitying, see:
O make our hearts Thy dwelling place,
And worthier Thee.

Harriet Auber
Hymn to the Holy Ghost

Et in Spiritum Sanctum, Dominum

I believe in the Holy Spirit,
the Lord, the giver of life,
who proceeds from the Father and the Son,
who with the Father and the Son
is adored and glorified,
who has spoken through the prophets.

Come, Holy Spirit, come!
And from your celestial home
Shed a ray of light divine!
Come, Father of the poor!
Come, source of all our store!
Come, within our bosoms shine.

Page 79:
The Holy Spirit *(17th century)*
Church of Santo Domingo, Puebla, Mexico

Faithful to scriptural and iconographical tradition, the dove of the Spirit characteristically spreads its wings, radiating the brilliance of its presence and splendor. The surrounding inscription evokes the primordial role of the Holy Spirit in salvation history and at the Incarnation: "The spirit of the Lord shall rest upon him" (Is 11:2). These golden rays streaming out in all directions recall the universality of his presence, the fire of his love, the power of the One whom nothing can contain, whom no one knows from whence he comes or where he is going. This Baroque representation communicates dynamism and vitality itself, which the Spirit offers to those who welcome him.

The Creed of Nicea, from the year 325, had only one sentence in the third article: "And in the Holy Spirit." At that time, the Church's teaching on the Holy Spirit had not yet been clarified. Controversy about the Holy Spirit broke out only around the year 360. Confusion and obscurity reigned; Saint Gregory Nazianzen famously commented on the understanding of the Holy Spirit in that era, that it was "a point on which to be only slightly in error was to be orthodox." By the time of the Council of Constantinople in 381, however, the Church's teaching, guided especially by Saint Athanasius of Alexandria and Saint Basil of Caesarea, was clarified, and the fathers at Constantinople composed this full article on the Holy Spirit. At the same time, however, they did not want to affirm more than was necessary, so as not to further divide an already divided Church. Thus, while the Creed speaks explicitly of the Son as "true God" and "consubstantial with the Father," neither term is used of the Holy Spirit. Instead, the same teaching is asserted by indirection.

The article begins, "I believe in the Holy Spirit, the Lord, the giver of life." In the Holy Scriptures, "Lord" is a title for God. So when the Creed calls the Holy "Spirit Lord", it is calling him God. And "giver of life" asserts the same thing. In Greek logic, one could give only what one had by nature. But if the Holy Spirit gives life, he has life by nature—that is, he is always alive, always existing. But what is always alive, what exists eternally, is God, and only God.

The Creed continues, "Who proceeds from the Father." The Creed had called the Son "the Only Begotten" and said that he was "begotten, not made." The fathers needed a word to

Tommaso di Giovanni Cassai, known as Masaccio (1401-c. 1428), ***The Trinity*** *(1425-1428)*
fresco, 263 x 125 in., Florence, Church of Santa Maria Novella

From his perspective within a trompe-l'oeil chapel, God the Father holds out between his hands the body of his Son nailed to the cross. But if this is the Trinity, where is the Holy Spirit? Quite simply and naturally, at the midpoint between their two faces, the body and wings of the dove appear—though from our perspective, at a distance, they seem only to form the neckline of the Father's voluminous tunic What a beautiful symbol! Through this fresco by Masaccio, a pioneer of artistic innovation in Renaissance Florence, we join in contemplation with the Virgin Mary (whose direct gaze and hand gesture invites our presence), Saint John, and the two patrons who commissioned the work—for the first time in art, represented in correct proportion to the sacred figures themselves. We join all of them, visually, thanks to the artist's perfect mastery of perspective.

même Jésus reviendra"
répandrai mon Esprit... Quiconque

describe the Holy Spirit's origin in the Father. They could not call him begotten, for then he would be a second Son. Saint Gregory Nazianzen expressed the idea concisely: "The Holy Spirit is truly Spirit, coming forth from the Father indeed, but not after the manner of the Son, for it is not by generation but by procession, since I must coin a word for the sake of clearness." Thus Gregory introduced the term "procession" to describe the origin of the Holy Spirit; he drew on a phrase in Saint John's Gospel, "the Spirit of truth, who proceeds from the Father" (Jn 15:26).

"Who proceeds from the Father and the Son." The words "and the Son" are one word in Latin, *Filioque*. This one word is the most contentious word in the Creed. It was not present in the original, composed in Greek in 381. The Latin church added it to the Creed around the tenth century. It presents Saint Augustine of Hippo's understanding of the Trinitarian processions. The Orthodox church rejects the addition. This ancient controversy cannot be solved here; we can only say that the Western understanding of the Holy Spirit sees him as the bond of love between the Father and the Son.

"Who spoke through the prophets." The second-century heretic Marcion has already been mentioned. This phrase in the third article of the Creed is the Church's final judgment on Marcion: the one God, the Father of our Lord Jesus Christ, is also the God who spoke through the prophets, and in the whole Old Testament. The Church cannot reject its Old Testament, the Jewish scriptures adopted by the Church and interpreted in light of Jesus Christ. God made a true covenant with the Jews, and it has not been abrogated.

Sylvie Gaudin (1950-1994), ***Pentecost*** *(1992-1994)*
stained glass, Church of Saint-Gervais, Paris

It's a veritable bonfire! Fire in the form of crackling, licking flames seeking only to consume everything in its path. But this is not a threatening, destructive blaze. It is divine fire: that of the Holy Spirit, who proceeds from the Father. In the center, can we not glimpse in what looks like a fluted pillar, the column of cloud that signified God's presence among his people? The letter Omega on the right tells us that the Spirit has been sent by God to guide us to the end of time. In this ultimate work in a cycle of five stained-glass windows, the artist's palette, as well as the vivacity of diverse shapes and textures, calls to mind the dynamic of baptism. Plunged into the Paschal Mystery, we are reborn through the waters of baptism (blue) as children of God. The Spirit (yellow) leads us into a Trinitarian communion of love. This path of faith proceeds through moments of hope (green) as well as doubt and obstacles (brown and black), as we are drawn into this ineffable vortex of superabundant life.

Francesco Castelli, known as Borromini (1599-1667), **Dome** *(1665-1667)*
86.6 x 53.3 ft., Church of San Carlo alle Quattro Fontane, Rome

By nature, the Holy Spirit is he who cannot be seen or grasped. It was the great genius of Borromini to depict him here at the center of the dazzling dome of this Roman church. For, by placing the Spirit at the summit of the dome lantern, he has lit upon the most effective way to confirm belief "in the Holy Spirit, the Lord, the giver of life." For is light not the ultimate source of life? And then there is the complex assemblage of the coffered ceiling—with all its various shapes no less significant in originality of design and dynamism. The cross, symbol of salvation, is juxtaposed to an octagon, an evocation of the Resurrection of the Son. Thus the architect splinters light into a prism of metaphors for the life-giving action of this Spirit who "proceeds from the Father and the Son." This underlying principle is further accentuated by the dove of the Spirit spreading his wings in the center of a triangle, a direct reference to the Holy Trinity.

"Who with the Father and the Son is adored and glorified." This clause reinforces the Church's confession that the Holy Spirit is equal in divinity to the Father and the Son: we adore the Holy Spirit as we do the Father and the Son, and the Holy Spirit is no less God than they are.

Thus, this one sentence presents, with beautiful concision, the Church's essential teaching on the Holy Spirit. The Holy Spirit is true God, as the Father and the Son are. He has his origin in the Father, and proceeds from both, or, as it is sometimes expressed, proceeds from the Father through the Son. And the Holy Spirit is the source of inspiration, for the Scriptures and for the Church. Each year, from Ascension Thursday to Pentecost Sunday, the Church makes a novena of prayer, asking for a new outpouring of the Holy Spirit. ■

Next page:
Michelangelo Buonarroti, known as Michelangelo (1475-1564),
Ezekiel *(1510), fresco, 140 x 149.6 in., Sistine Chapel, Rome*

Prophets incarnate the urgent need to communicate the divine message and the intense desire to be obedient to God's voice. This is powerfully depicted here by Michelangelo on the ceiling of the Sistine Chapel. Of course, Ezekiel is emphatically aware of his prophetic mission: his imposing stature and two feet planted solidly on the ground attest to that. But the artist's great genius lies in his ability to interpret how the eruption of the glory of God transformed this priest into a prophetic preacher of salvation. In contemplating him, we truly have the impression of entering into the dialogue between the prophet—his face straining, his eyes piercing and attentive—and the "voice" depicted in the form of an angel who inspires his words, or, at any rate, indicates their origin by pointing up to the heavens. In the cycle of The Prophets *in the Sistine Chapel, the artist's visualization is a reflection of these men's states of mind—sometimes bright, sometimes somber—men who proclaimed and sought to penetrate the promise of the Messiah through divine inspiration, personified by one or two small figures placed next to each one of them. Thus, Michelangelo sets himself apart from traditional representations of this Spirit who continues to speak to us in the intimacy of our hearts.*

SANCTISS·TRINITATI·BEATOQ·CAROLO·BORROMEO·D·AN·SAL·M·DC·XL

How Great a Cloud of Witnesses

And as a little baby lifts his arms
to mama when he's filled with milk, and shows
the kindling of the love within his soul,

So did those splendors stand with wings that rose
pointing their flames unto the highest height
and making manifest how great their love

For Mary was. They stood before my sight,
singing the "Queen of Heaven" with sound so sweet,
my memory yet treasures the delight.

O what a fertile harvest of fine wheat
is crammed into those bins in richest measure,
who here on earth were such good fields to sow!

Here do they live, here they enjoy the treasure
they won with tears they wept in Babylon,
in exile, when they left the gold in scorn.

Here triumphs under the exalted Son
of God and Son of Mary, for his victory,
with both the ancient council and the new,
the one who keeps the keys to such great glory.

Dante
describing the Church Triumphant
and his meeting with Saint Peter and the Apostles,
in *Paradiso*

Et unam, sanctam, catholicam et apostolicam Ecclesiam

I believe in one, holy,
catholic and apostolic Church.

Lord, be with your people.
Simon the fisherman was called by you to be a fisher of men:
call others today to share in his task.
When the disciples feared that the ship was sinking,
you commanded the sea and there was calm:
protect your Church in the midst of trouble,
and give her the peace that the world cannot give.

IC
XC

Page 89:
The Master of Cabestany, ***The Appearance of Christ to Two Disciples*** *(c. 1175), marble, 31.9 x 24.4 x 7.1 in.*

How the bark of Peter is tossed about in the passage from the Gospel of Mark (4:35-41)! Just as the bark of the Church still is today! But I believe in her; the Savior will come to her just as he does here to the two disciples rowing for their lives. With touching details added to the somewhat schematic style of the time, this low relief carving expresses the hardships of navigation. The men are too busy avoiding shipwreck on these wild seas to take notice of the waters below teeming with fish. Peter, straining to put all his effort into the task, supports his weight with his foot propped on the prow of the boat. In response to his raised hand, symbol either of surprise or a call for help, comes the commanding gesture of Christ who alone can calm the storm. He comes bearing peace, as the inscription on the cover of the Book of Life he holds makes clear: Pax vobis.

We say "I believe in one God. . . ," "I believe in one Lord Jesus Christ. . . ," "I believe in the Holy Spirit. . . ," without hesitation. But what does it mean to say, "I believe in one. . . Church"? I am a member, a part, of the Church. Saint Robert Bellarmine had famously said, "The Church is as visible as the Kingdom of France or the Republic of Venice," in response to the Protestant Reformers' assertion that the Church was purely spiritual and invisible. Am I making an act of faith in myself?

Yes, the Church is visible—gathered before the altar on Sunday morning—but it is also invisible, a mystery constituted by God's grace. Pope John Paul II's last encyclical was entitled *Ecclesia de Eucharistia*, "The Church draws her life from the Eucharist." The Eucharist is the sacramental Body of Christ, and the Church is the Mystical Body of Christ. Thus we can make an act of faith in the Church, for the Church is something beyond us and above us. As Vatican II taught, "the Church is the Reign of Christ already

Greek School, ***The Holy Apostles Peter and Paul*** *(16th century) tempera on wood, 21.6 x 17 in.*

Jesus, Peter, and Paul—the very foundations of the Church are presented here in this "sacred conversation," at one and the same time atemporal—eternal even, as the Byzantine gold background confirms—and current. For what they hold out in this scale model of a central-plan church enshrining the altar of the Eucharistic sacrifice is the manifestation of the presence of the Risen One himself. Two large figures, in classical clothing accentuated by a satiny sheen, present to the Lord this place of worship. By their gaze, Peter—who received the keys to the kingdom—and Paul—who addressed his epistles to the faithful exhorting them to enter into a new relationship with God through faith in Jesus Christ—seem to invite us to join them in this "presentation." Our attachment to the Church is as though encouraged by Jesus himself: emerging out of the sky, he blesses the two Apostles, and urges us to recognize its indissoluble link with the One who is the very source of the sanctity of the Church.

present in mystery" (*Lumen Gentium*, 3).

Some Fathers of the Church contemplated the birth of the Church from the pierced side of Christ on the cross: just as Eve was born from the side of the sleeping Adam, so the Church came forth from the side of the dead Christ, in water and blood, the sacraments of baptism and the Eucharist. Others looked to the first Pentecost as the birthday of the Church, when the Holy Spirit came down upon the disciples in tongues of fire. The Creed places the act of faith in the Church in the third article, on the Holy Spirit. The Holy Spirit bestows his gifts on the Church: wisdom, understanding, counsel, fortitude, knowledge, piety, and fear of the Lord.

The Church is also called the People of God, "a chosen race, a royal priesthood, a holy nation, a people for your own possession," as the liturgy has it. One becomes a member of the People of God by faith and baptism; its head is Jesus Christ. The law of this people is the New Commandment of love.

In the creeds of the early centuries, several terms were used to describe the Church. The Creed of Constantinople gathered all of them, four in number, and applied them to the Church: the Church is one, holy, catholic, and apostolic. Each attribute should be considered.

The Church is one. She is one because of her source and origin, the one God. She is one because of her founder, the one Lord Jesus Christ. She is one because of her soul, the Holy Spirit. Thus she is one in the Trinity. The Church is also one in her profession of the one faith, received from the Apostles, one in the celebration of Eucharistic worship, and one in apostolic succession, the college of bishops under the pope.

Yet the Church's unity is not uniformity. Her liturgy is celebrated in different rites—Roman, Byzantine, Armenian, and others—and, since Vatican II, the Roman rite Mass is celebrated in hundreds of different languages. The Church's members live out their call in different ways: in marriage, as clergy, as vowed religious.

Vatican II taught that the one Church of Christ subsists in the Catholic Church under the successor of Peter and the bishops in communion with

Caspar David Friedrich (1774-1840), ***The Cathedral*** *(c. 1818)*
oil on canvas, 60 x 27.8 in.

Let me guide you through this flight into an often inaccessible distant world, this surprising dreamland, this awe-inspiring apparition into which Friedrich invites us. As believers, we are the Church, the Body of the risen Christ. The members of this Body gather in the church, the temple where we meet and receive God made manifest in the sacraments. Here, the lofty forms and the verticality of the façade articulate in and of themselves the visibility, the universality, the importance of its presence in our world. This imposing Gothic cathedral—a style particularly in vogue in nineteenth-century northern Europe—seems to float in the clouds. Angels adore the Eucharistic presence. The monstrance in the shape of a cross, its heart throbbing with a supernatural glow, is surmounted by a rainbow, the biblical symbol of the covenant. Like these soaring towers, pinnacles, and spires, we strain upward toward him with our whole being to experience the fullness of his presence and his love. Just as this church is bathed in supernatural light, am I, as a member of the Church, not also immersed in the light of divine love?

Piero della Francesca (c. 1416-1492), **The Madonna of Mercy** *(1455-1460)*
tempera and gold leaf on wood, 52.8 x 35.8 in.

Based on a medieval iconographical tradition, Mary is represented here as the personification of the Church—Mother Church, who welcomes us, whoever we are and whatever our background. Once more, the miracle of art reunites us with the people in this scene. Mary opens her maternal arms to me, not only to give me refuge close to her but to protect me, along with all those who have already taken their place within the ample folds of the mantle she opens out to us. For, as we well know, our faith demands to be nurtured, strengthened, and constantly defended from attack. In this spiritual combat, the Church is sanctified as the privileged repository of the Good News which she proclaims and manifests, as does Mary here. Hers is the gentle idealized face and the solidity of a draped body which detracts not in the least from the sense of peace and blessing she communicates to us. Her whole being suggests a little chapel formed by this column of a body on which her cloak hangs like a dome lightly supported over the arches of her arms.

him. But there are also other churches, such as the Orthodox, which possess the fullness of sacramental life; and ecclesial communities of Protestants, with valid baptism, the treasure of the Holy Scriptures, and a life of faith, hope, and charity.

The Church is holy. Holiness is, before all else, an attribute of God. "Be holy, for I am holy," we read again and again, especially in the Book of Leviticus. Holiness implies separateness, especially from all that is sordid or sinful. But by his love for his Bride, Christ communicates his holiness to the Church. And the holy Church both calls her members to holiness and bestows holiness upon them, especially through the sacraments. No member of the Church claims to be without sin. But the Church may acknowledge, after their deaths, that some believers lived lives of heroic and exemplary holiness and canonize them as saints.

The Church is catholic. "Catholic" means universal, and the Church is catholic in a double sense. As the Body of Christ, she is united with her Head, and she has received from Christ the fullness of the means of salvation—the faith, the sacraments, and ordained ministry—so that she offers the means of salvation to all. Then too, the Church is catholic because Christ has sent her to preach the saving Gospel to the whole human race. Those who accept the gift of faith are members of a particular church, under a bishop; and each of these particular churches is in communion with the church of Rome, and thus with each other.

The Church is apostolic. The Church was founded on the Apostles, the men who accompanied Jesus from the baptism of John until the Ascension (see Acts 1:21–22), and who were witnesses of the Resurrection. The testimony of the Apostles is preserved for all time in the New Testament. And their office as apostles is carried on by the college of bishops, ordained to that office in unbroken succession down the centuries. Thus every Christian, even in the most remote corners of the world, is in communion of faith and life with "the twelve apostles of the Lamb" (Rv 21:14). And every Christian is called to be apostolic, that is, to proclaim the saving Gospel of Jesus Christ. ■

Next page:
Roman School, ***View of Saint Peter's Square in Rome*** *(1665)*
oil on canvas

This seventeenth-century view reveals the imposing layout of Saint Peter's Square shortly after its completion. Two gigantic wings reach out in a welcoming embrace. Here is the sign of the universality of the Church, gathering as one to her heart the faithul in all their diversity. Here is its splendid architectural manifestation in the vast colonnade of Saint Peter's Square designed by Gian Lorenzo Bernini. This is the view which for over four centuries has greeted pilgrims who come to pray at the tomb of Saint Peter. Even before entering the basilica, they are awed by the multitude of statues of the saints who seem to watch over them and guide them. With emotion, they consider the obelisk in the center of the square which witnessed the martyrdom of the Apostle Peter. The theatricality typical of the Baroque period further heightens the imposing array of two hundred and eighty-four Doric columns recalling that my faith is rooted in the witness of the Apostles, the great pillars of the Church. May my faith remain as solid as these stones. . .

IN HONOREM PRIN. APOSTO

ESIUS ROMAN V ANNO DNI MDCXX

Born Anew

Since, Lord, to Thee
A narrow way and little gate
Is all the passage, on my infancy
Thou didst lay hold, and antedate
My faith in me.

O let me still
Write Thee great God, and me a child:
Let me be soft and supple to Thy will,
Small to myself, to others mild,
Behither ill.

Although by stealth
My flesh get on, yet let her sister
My soul bid nothing, but preserve her wealth:
The growth of flesh is but a blister;
Childhood is health.

George Herbert
From "Holy Baptism"

Confiteor unum baptisma

I confess one Baptism for the forgiveness of sins

May the power of the Holy Spirit,
O Lord, we pray,
come down through your Son
into the fullness of this font,
so that all who have been buried with Christ
by Baptism into death
may rise again to life with him.

Baptism in the first of the seven sacraments, the basis of the whole Christian life and the gateway to life in the Spirit. So the Creed rightly mentions baptism immediately after the Church. As a sacrament, baptism is a sign —that is, a reality known first that leads to knowledge of another reality. It is a specific kind of sign, a symbol: a reality that in itself points to a meaning, but to which a deeper meaning has been added by the one who instituted it. Washing with water is itself a sign of cleansing. But when he instituted the sacrament of baptism, Christ added a far deeper meaning to the washing, namely, the forgiveness of all sins.

Christ instituted the sacrament of baptism after his Resurrection, when he encountered the Eleven on a mountain in Galilee and said to them, "All authority in heaven and on earth has been given to me. Go therefore and make disciples of all nations, baptizing them in

Previous page:
Bicci di Lorenzo (1373-1452),
The Baptism of Saint Pancras,
tempera and gold leaf on wood, 27 x 20.6 in.

According to legend, Saint Pancras was baptized as a young man along with his uncle Dionysius by the bishop of Rome, Saint Cornelius. They were probably martyred under Emperor Diocletian (early fourth century). Let us admire the composition: in a setting inspired by Quattrocento baptistery architecture, the celebrant, wearing a miter and cape of gold, pours water over the catechumen's head, under the eyes of his uncle. Pancras, humbly kneeling, is unclothed, divested of his former life. We can just make out the baptismal font in the background. One assistant holds the paschal candle, another a fresh vestment—two symbols of new life in Christ.

the name of the Father and of the Son and of the Holy Spirit, teaching them to observe all that I have commanded you" (Mt 28:18–20).

The sacrament of baptism is celebrated many times throughout the year, often on Sunday. But the archetypal moment for the celebration of baptism, especially the baptism of adults, is the Easter Vigil. The new fire has been blessed, and the Easter Gospel has been sung. Christ has been given new and exalted life; and now, the candidates for baptism will also enter into new and eternal life. In the early Church, some baptismal fonts were rectangular, in the shape of a grave. Candidates stepped down into the font, advancing from west, the symbol of darkness and evil, to east, the symbol of light and life. Going down to death and rising again recalls Saint Paul's words: "Do you not know that all of us who were baptized into Christ Jesus were baptized into his death? We were buried therefore with him

Lorenzo Ghiberti (1378-1455)
***The Gates of Paradise** (1421)*
bronze bas-relief, 236 x 182 in.,
East door, Baptistery of Saint John, Florence, Italy

The beauty and imposing presence of much of the episcopal architecture of Italy—and particularly of Florence—enables us to once again experience the profound meaning of our baptism. In the early history of the Church, adults alone were baptized on the feast of Easter. Catechumens were allowed to enter the cathedral only to listen to the bishop's catechesis. The baptistery was a separate space reserved for catechumens to receive the sacrament. Only then would they cross the parvis and enter the sanctuary to take part for the first time in the Eucharist. Here in Florence, the newly baptized would exit through these sumptuous doors, appropriately named for their function as "the gates of paradise." Was I too not baptized to gain access into the fullness of divine life? The episodes from the Old Testament depicted on these ten bronze panels remind us of the Lord's untiring fidelity and his repeated calls to a covenant with him.

Baptistery *(5th century), Saint-Sauveur Cathedral, Aix-en-Provence, France*

"The old things have passed away; behold, new things have come" (2 Cor 5:17). These paschal words of Saint Paul aptly evoke the very particular atmosphere that this building radiates, which dates to the fifth-century (with the exception of the upper-level Baroque additions). In the heart of the city, a new community constructed this baptistery as the catechumens' final destination on their spiritual journey to the first sacrament of Christian initiation. Using architectural elements salvaged from the debris of the most beautiful pagan monuments, the result is a harmoniously integrated octagon surmounted by a dome. The symbolism is clear: the number eight evokes the Resurrection, while the semi-circular dome suggests the heavens, the Kingdom of God, and divine perfection. The ring of columns with its arcade of rounded arches sets off to great effect another octagon: that of the baptismal pool in which the catechumen would be immersed.

by baptism into death, so that as Christ was raised from the dead by the glory of the Father, we too might walk in newness of life" (Rom 6:3–4). When they emerged from the font, the newly baptized were given white garments, for they had "put on Christ" (Gal 3:27).

The condition for baptism is faith. "Believe in the Lord Jesus, and you will be saved" (Acts 16:21), Saint Paul said to his jailer in Philippi. The jailer and his family believed, and they were baptized. In the rite of baptism, the profession of the Creed precedes the administration of the sacrament.

In the early Church, an extended preparation for baptism gradually evolved. In some cases, the preparation began with a three-year period of instruction and examination. The more immediate preparation began about six weeks before Easter, a time of rigorous fasting, daily exorcisms, and catechesis on the Creed. In some places, candidates were given the Creed and the Lord's Prayer during these weeks and required to memorize them. The baptisms took place during the Easter Vigil, as the community spent the entire night in the church, praying, singing, listening to the Scriptures, and waiting for the moment of sunrise, when the Eucharistic liturgy of Easter began. Since Vatican II, the Rite of Christian Initiation for Adults has restored some of the elements of this ancient practice.

The effects of baptism are far-reaching. The sacrament brings

Next page:
Francisco de Zurbarán (1598-1664), ***Agnus Dei*** *(1635-1640)*
oil on canvas, 14.7 x 24.4 in.

Isaiah prophesied that the Suffering Servant of the Lord would take the place of the paschal victim, silent and defenseless, brought before his executioners like a lamb to the slaughter. He foretold that this Servant would be a victim whose sacrifice saves us from sin and death. And this lamb has always served as the image of Christ giving his life for the forgiveness of sins. He will utter not a word. This same destitution, this same consent, silent and resigned, is revealed in this lamb, its feet tethered, lying on a table. Nothing else. No bright color relieves the palette of black and gray with tints of burnt sienna. Through this economy of means the form of the animal is revealed in all its purity. The Lamb of God submits. Its bound feet leave no doubt as to its ultimately violent destiny. Its eyes are lost in impenetrable thought. Its soft fleece is revealed in the purity of a splendid shaft of light. In the face of such self-surrender, how can we not but be deeply moved?

Francesco Trevisani (1656-1746), ***Peter Baptizes Cornelius the Centurion*** *(1709)*
oil on canvas, 28.1 x 17.9 in.

Here is one of the most important episodes recounted in the Acts of the Apostles (10:1-49). Cornelius was a devout Roman centurion who constantly prayed to God. Through the intervention of an angel of the Lord, Peter visited Cornelius in his house in Caesarea to tell him of the Good News he had received from the Lord. According to the biblical account, "the Holy Spirit fell upon all those who were listening to the word." Here, an imposing and solemn Peter, in timeless dress, baptizes the soldier who humbly kneels. His helmet placed before him, he is still wearing his breastplate and cloak, symbols of the authority of Roman power and a reminder of his historical roots. Baptismal immersion gives way here to a trickle of water upon the head, which was to become the more common rite in the Christian West.

about the forgiveness of all sins, the guilt of original sin and all personal sins. It is birth into a new life by the grace of divine adoption, incorporation into the Body of Christ, and becoming a temple of the Holy Spirit. The baptized become members of the Church and sharers in the priesthood of all believers.

Baptism also imprints on the soul what the Christian tradition calls an indelible spiritual sign, or a character. The indelible character is the reason why the Creed speaks of "one" baptism: the sacrament of baptism can be received only once, and it cannot be repeated. This point was worked out at length by Saint Augustine in the early fifth century; it is to the same bishop of Hippo that we owe much of the theology of the sacraments. Opponents of his, the Donatists, insisted that Catholic baptism was invalid, so they "rebaptized" Catholics who became Donatists. Augustine held that baptism, no matter where it was administered, was valid, so long as water was poured and the Trinity was invoked. But the sacrament was precisely a sign, and only a sign. The reality that the sign pointed to was charity, or sanctifying grace, which was given only in the Catholic Church. So Augustine did not "rebaptize" Donatists who became Catholics, but simply recognized their incorporation into the Church. The same principle is applied today: baptized Protestants who enter full communion with the Catholic Church are not baptized, but given Confirmation and the Holy Eucharist upon their reception.

He Is Risen Indeed!

Enough! The Resurrection,
A heart's clarion! Across my foundering deck shone
A beacon, an eternal beam! Flesh fade, and mortal trash
Fall to the residuary worm; world's wildfire, leave but ash:
In a flash, at a trumpet's crash,
I am all at once what Christ is, since He was what I am, and
This Jack, joke, poor potsherd, patch, matchwood, immortal diamond
Is immortal diamond.

Gerard Manley Hopkins
From "That Nature is a Heraclitean Fire,
and the Glory of the Resurrection"

ET EXSPECTO RESURRECTIONEM MORTUORUM

and I look forward to the resurrection of the dead

But as for me, I know that my Vindicator lives,
and that he will at last stand forth upon the dust;
And from my flesh I shall see God;
my inmost being is consumed with longing.

Previous page:
Nicolas of Verdun (1130-c. 1205), ***The Resurrection of the Dead*** *(1181)*
enamel on gilded copper, 8.1 x 6.5 in., Abbey Church of Klosterneuburg, Austria

After the great silence, the stillness, and the chill of the tomb comes the great moment of awakening, of a veritable upheaval. The technique of champlevé, or "raised field," enameling, perfectly mastered by the medieval period, is here placed at the service of the message. Angels burst from above, their bodies perfectly molded to the contours of the frame, while those once dead hurry to rise from their tombs. In one great surging movement, the heavy stone lids of the tombs seem as light as feathers! The outstretched arms call to mind those of newborn babes reaching out to those who gave them life. The resurrection is truly a new birth when night gives way to day. The Latin inscription surrounding this finely-executed element of an altarpiece is taken from the Book of Daniel: "Many of those who sleep in the dust of the earth shall awake" (12:2).

We believe that, on the last day, Christ will raise our bodies from the dead, and we will, body and soul, live with him for ever. Ancient pagans found this belief curious, or absurd. The sophisticated men of Athens listened to Saint Paul until he mentioned the resurrection of the dead, and then they walked away in disdain; we read in Acts, "now when they heard of the resurrection of the dead, some mocked; but others said, 'We will hear you again about this'" (Acts 17:32).

But the Christian faith is clear: Jesus Christ was raised from the dead on the first Easter Sunday, and our resurrection is a consequence of his. The Apostle writes: "Now if Christ is preached as raised from the dead, how can some of you say that there is no resurrection of the dead? But if there is no resurrection of the dead, then Christ has not been raised; if Christ has not been raised, then our preaching is in vain and your faith is in vain" (1 Cor 15:12–14). Jesus himself attests to this hope when he says, "I am the resurrection and the life" (Jn 11:25).

How the resurrection of the dead will take place is deeply mysterious. In death, the soul is separated from the body and goes to meet God, and to stand before Christ in judgment. The body of a Christian, which has been a temple of the Holy Spirit, is brought to the parish church. Mass is celebrated for the dead person, and the body is honored with holy water and incense. It

Wassily Kandinsky (1866-1944), ***The Last Judgment*** *(1910)*
oil on canvas

I can hear it, that trumpet awakening all those slumbering in the tomb. Its blast booms like a roar of thunder, for the person in the foreground is covering his ears. The warm color and characteristic shape of the trumpet fills the entire center of the canvas, relegating the face of the musician-angel to the upper right-hand corner. Music itself is intrinsic to the subject here since, according to Kandinsky, it is the ideal model of high art inviting the artist to "compose" in tune with "rhythmic and melodic" methods. Colors play the role of musical notes. The juxtaposition of flat patches of color give the impression of accelerando—a quickening movement, from a cold palette through to warmer tones. An accumulation of shapes deconstructs the space. The absence of fixed points of reference draws the eye into a truly vibrant crescendo echoing the strident trumpet blast. The dead one will leave the cocoon in which he had been isolated and forgotten. Upon hearing the call of the divine messenger, the flesh-tinged hue of life begins once more to seep into his limbs.

NDINSKY 1910

The Mausoleum of Galla Placidia *(5th century), Ravenna, Italy*

This was to be the final resting place of Galla Placidia who had this mausoleum built around the year 430. Her position as empress explains the magnificence of this tomb. Who could remain unmoved by the intensity of these mosaics: the star-studded sky filling the upper register, or the sparkling abstract and vegetal motifs garlanding the underside of the arches? All combine to make of this waiting room of the resurrection a witness to firm hope. The feeling of harmony and serenity emanating from this tomb accompanies the visitor in a meditation that urges us to join in prayer with all those awaiting the resurrection that will immerse them and us in endless light.

is then, usually at least, buried in consecrated ground. There it decays and returns to the earth from which it was taken (see Gn 3:19).

The risen body will be in a new and different state. We read that Jesus raised Lazarus from the dead. As Saint John portrays the scene, Lazarus returned home to his sisters, resumed his life with them, and eventually died again, in his old age. The risen body of Christ received a higher kind of existence, and Saint Paul assures us that we will, too: "So it is with the resurrection of the dead. What is sown is perishable, what is raised is imperishable. . . . It is sown a physical body, it is raised a spiritual body" (1 Cor 15:42, 44).

What precedes the resurrection of the dead is death, and our faith offers us a Christian understanding of death. That understanding has two aspects. One is negative: death as we know it, with its ugliness, pain, and sorrow, is a consequence of sin. God forbade Adam and Eve to eat of one tree in the garden, saying, "In the day that you eat of it you shall die" (Gn 2:17). Saint Paul calls death "the last enemy" of man, which is still to be destroyed (see 1 Cor 15:26). But because Christ died, and died for us, Christian death also has a positive meaning. In a mysterious way, our own death participates in Christ's death: "If we have died with him, we shall also live with him" (2 Tm 2:11). In baptism, we have already entered into Christ's death and already have a new life in him. The funeral liturgy expresses this mystery beautifully: "for your faithful, Lord, life is changed not ended, and, when this earthly dwelling turns to dust, an eternal dwelling is made ready for them in heaven."

Life is a good and beautiful gift, and there is no wrong in fearing death. But our faith gives us confidence that death is not the end of all, and we pray for the opportunity to prepare well for death. We ask Mary often, "pray for us sinners, now and at the hour of our death." ■

Next page:
Joseph Mallord William Turner (1775-1851), ***The Angel Standing in the Sun*** *(1846)*
oil on canvas, 31 x 31 in.

It is a veritable blaze. This alone is enough to signal the talent of the English master whose splendid sunsets we have become accustomed to. But here, it is not a question of twilight. Is it a destructive fire? A call to life? Is this an angel of the light or of the shades (the two scenes at his feet depict Adam and Eve mourning over Abel and the tragic episode of Judith and Holofernes)? The artist draws his inspiration from the Book of Revelation: "Then I saw an angel standing on the sun. He cried out in a loud voice to all the birds flying high overhead, 'Come here. Gather for God's great feast'" (Rv 19:17). Here, earthly and heavenly time is united. In this whirlwind of light, we discover that the end of time will be the end of History, when the elect will enter into life without end. As inscribed on the canvas, cosmic chaos here becomes "the morning march that flashes to the sun."

We Shall See Him Face to Face

Pleasant are Thy courts above
In the land of light and love;
Pleasant are Thy courts below
In this land of sin and woe:
O, my spirit longs and faints
For the converse of Thy saints,
For the brightness of Thy face,
For Thy fullness, Lord of grace.

Happy birds that sing and fly
Round Thy altars, O most High;
Happier souls that find a rest
In a heavenly Father's breast!
Like the wandering dove that found
No repose on earth around,
They can to their ark repair,
And enjoy it ever there.

Happy souls, their praises flow
Even in this vale of woe;
Waters in the desert rise,
Manna feeds them from the skies;
On they go from strength to strength,
Till they reach Thy throne at length,
At Thy feet adoring fall,
Who hast led them safe through all.

Lord, be mine this prize to win,
Guide me through a world of sin,
Keep me by Thy saving grace,
Give me at Thy side a place;
Sun and shield alike Thou art,
Guide and guard my erring heart,
Grace and glory flow from Thee;
Shower, O shower them, Lord, on me.

Henry Lyte
From "Pleasant Are Thy Courts Above"

Et vitam venturi saeculi

and the life of the world to come.

*The glory of God is man fully alive,
and the life of man is the vision of God.*

Previous page:
The Good Shepherd *(late 3rd–early 4th century)*
marble, 39.4 x 14.2 x 10.6 in.

From the earliest days of the Church, Christians have adopted the figure of the Good Shepherd to witness to the hope of their faith. Jesus referred to himself as such (Jn 10:11) and told the parable of the shepherd who goes off in search of the lost sheep (Lk 15:3-7). This young beardless shepherd is Christ bearing salvation and offering eternal life to the departed dead, for he "gives his life for his sheep."

Hieronymus Bosch (1450-1516), ***Ascent to the Empyrean*** *(1500-1504)*
oil on wood, 34 x 15.5 in., Doge's Palace, Venice

Hieronymus Bosch invites us into a veritable mystical experience. Through this astonishing early sixteenth-century painting, worthy inspiration for future surrealists or science fiction movies, he describes the indescribable.
In the middle of nowhere, emerging from vaporous clouds, angels escort the elect. As though drawn by a supernatural light, they cannot fail to be stunned and dazzled. Even the angels succumb to the power of love and peace irresistibly beckoning them upward. This vision transports us into the heart of the artist's imagination. Such spiraling into an infinite well of light is the materialization of God's promise to us. One delicate silhouette is already contemplating the unveiling of this gift. In this earthly existence, we must carry on hoping and believing, doing everything in our power to cross that threshold, the culmination of all existence—that we may finally see, and finally live!

"And the life of the world to come." Death is not the end of all; it is not annihilation. The Creed invites us to faith in life that goes on after the death of the body. The Creed speaks of a "world to come." The Apocalypse of John speaks of "a new heaven and a new earth" (Rv 21:1). In a mysterious way, the world will not be destroyed but renewed. In our final state, we read, "the dwelling of God is with men" (Rv 21:3).

The Creed uses the word "life" twice. Once is here, in the promise of the life of the world to come. The other is in the confession of faith in the Holy Spirit, who is designated the "giver of life," which means that he is alive by his nature, and therefore divine.

Much about the world to come is unknown or obscure, but some truths are revealed. At the moment of death all moral choices cease, and the particular judgment takes place. The way we lived our lives—choosing the good or choosing sin—marks our destiny for eternity. Those who die unrepentant in mortal sin have chosen an eternity separated from God for ever, a state that is called "hell." To deny that hell exists is, finally, to deny free choice. Those who die in God's grace and friendship are saved. They will live in heaven, in perfect beatitude, where they will see God face to face and be in communion of life and love with the Most Holy Trinity.

But some who die in God's grace and friendship but are

Pages 122 and 123:
Alfred Manessier (1911-1993), ***Alleluia*** *(1981),*
lithograph, 23.5 x 17 in.

The colors and juxtaposition of shapes are the source of the rhythm and dynamism of this work, a pulsating fluctuation between God and life. Against a blood-red background, life circulates through a network of white veins, uniting what are true explosions of color, from blue to orange by way of green. This is the joyful "Alleluia" cry of the believer in praise of his Lord. Thanks to the gridwork uniting these patterns, whose color becomes light, we plunge into this abstraction of a utopian landscape where the eye of the viewer and matter itself—and the interior experience it invites—merge into one.

not yet fully purified undergo a cleansing, in a state that the Church calls purgatory. The souls in purgatory cannot help themselves, because they can no longer merit, but our prayers and good works can help them. Thus we have the beautiful Catholic practice of praying for the dead, and especially of offering the

*Anonymous, **The Vision of the Heavenly Jerusalem** (late 11th century)*
Latin manuscript, 11.6 x 8.7 in.

"I also saw the holy city, a new Jerusalem, coming down out of heaven from God, prepared as a bride adorned for her husband" (Rv 21:2). The glory that awaits us defies description. God has become the true Temple for each one of us, just as we are the temples of his presence. The Lamb in the center is the perfect image of this presence which illumines our hearts. As described in John's vision (Rv 21:12-14), the new Jerusalem appears in a circle of twelve colored rings, surrounded by twelve gates facing in all four directions to give entrance to all peoples, nations, and tongues on earth. This explosion of color, the visual vocalization of that which cannot be put into words, ushers us into this renewed, transformed, and transfigured world.

Holy Sacrifice of the Mass on their behalf. The offering of the Requiem Mass is the richest aspect of the Catholic funeral liturgy: we have it offered for the dead in the firm confidence that it assists the souls in purgatory and hastens their entry into heaven. ■

*Éric Michel, **Infinity** (2012)*
blue neon sculpture, 16.9 x 8.3 x 5.1 in.

We rediscover light. It irradiates and envelops all who approach this work of art. The object itself is the source of this luminosity that emits an intense azure blue. This is no innocuous form: it is "infinity." Éric Michel makes use of the mathematician's symbol to conjure blessed eternity. Technology at the service of the sacred here culminates in the expression of the essential: the artistic vehicle becomes the message itself. No need for any further mediation, since the work itself diffuses the light which endows it with all its meaning. Contemporary art startles us, making a clean slate of all our normal criteria about conceptions and perceptions. Form, color, and matter in the raw are all that matters. It is up to us alone to feel, interpret, and know how it touches us. And the question posed here is one of the most fundamental. . .

épreuve d'artiste

I/XL

And God Shall Be All in All

Then do I think on that which Nature said,
Of that same time when no more change shall be,
But steadfast rest of all things firmly stayed
Upon the pillars of Eternity,
That is contraire to Mutability:
For all that moveth doth in change delight,
But thenceforth all shall rest eternally
With Him, that doth the God of Sabaoth hight:
O that great Sabaoth God, grant me that Sabbath's sight.

Edmund Spenser
From *The Faerie Queene*

AMEN.

Through him, and with him, and in him,
O God, almighty Father,
in the unity of the Holy Spirit,
all glory and honor is yours,
for ever and ever.

Previous page:
Auguste Gilbert Privat (1892-1969), ***The Prayer***
15.7 x 4.3 x 5.1 in.

A face emerges. . .the verticality of the composition which, like our relationship to God, makes us turn and rise up toward him who, completely Other, is also found deep within ourselves. For this is a face in meditation. Two joined hands, rising up from the base to support the entire sculpture, barely brush half-opened lips murmuring the words of a prayer from the depths of the heart. These slender fingers joined together and raised toward the heavens are the materialization of this prayer, like the veritable heartbeat of a soul. The breath that escapes this face, the large eyes focused on eternity—does it not say "Amen"? At the end of our Creed, would this not be the most peaceful of expressions, serene yet firm, of our profession of faith in the divine project? "Yes, truly, I believe. . ."

The Creed ends with the Hebrew word "amen." The word comes from the same Hebrew root as the word "believe," so that the Amen at the end of the Creed mirrors "I believe" at the beginning. "Amen" affirms both God's fidelity toward us and our trust in him.

A verse from the prophet Isaiah uses this Hebrew root twice, in two different senses. It reads, "If you will not believe, surely you will not be established" (Is 7:9). In this verse, "believe" and "establish" represent the same root, "amen." Faith gives us a sure place, a trustworthy home.

Saint Augustine used a somewhat different version of this verse: "Unless you shall have believed, you will not understand," and quoted it often in his writings. In his interpretation, belief or faith had to precede understanding or insight; once we accepted the Christian faith in humility, a world of understanding would open up to us.

Joseph Ratzinger-Pope Benedict XVI, in his famous book *Introduction to Christianity*, has yet another interpretation of the verse from Isaiah. Relying on the Hebrew sense of the word "amen," he understands it as "unless you take a stand, you will not understand"—that is, every one of us has a basic outlook on life, and from that outlook we interpret the whole world and all our experience.

So our Amen, our great Amen, is both the place where we stand and the faith that we profess. Both lead us to the truth of the one God whose name is Father, Son, and Holy Spirit, the Creed that we profess with trust and joy. ■

Giovanni di Paolo (c. 1399-1482), ***Paradise*** *(detail, 1445)*
tempera on wood, 18.5 x 16 in.

Eternal springtime in the garden of paradise regained. An idyllic vision, at once rustic and serene, in which peace and concord without end are the source of all action and emotion. In the shade of an orchard, limbs laden with fruit, on the lush carpet of a flowering glade where rabbits gambol freely, happy people of all ages and estates converse and embrace. Here a religious benefits from the tender witness of an angel, while there, lower down, two women seem to renew an old friendship long interrupted. Men and women, laypeople and religious, rich and poor, young and old—all find themselves reunited in this paradisiacal setting which in most things still strongly resembles what we know here below on earth. But this depiction is above all the expression of our hope for contentment, harmony, love. Is this not what we desire? Is this not what we yearn for in accord with the will of my God? This is what we proclaim in the "Amen" that we pronounce at the end of our profession of faith.

Index of Artists

Cover and page 58:
Guido di Pietro, in religion Fra Giovanni, later known as Fra Angelico (Vicchio di Mugello, c. 1401–Rome, 1455), was a painter of the Quattrocento. A Dominican friar, he sought to combine the use of perspective and the representation of the human form with religious themes and the mystical meaning of light.

Page 14:
Girolamo dai Libri (Verona, c. 1475–1555) was an Italian manuscript illuminator of the Veronese Renaissance, also known for his altarpieces.

Page 15:
Philippe de Champaigne (Brussels, 1602–Paris, 1674) was a painter of the Classical period. Close to the Jansenist movement, his exceptional life's work was principally religiously inspired.

Page 16:
Maurice Denis (Granville, 1870–Paris, 1943), a painter in the Nabis movement, was also a designer, printmaker, and art theoretician. A Third Order Dominican, he was devoted to the recognition of Christian art.

Page 20:
Auguste Rodin (Paris, 1840–Meudon, 1917) was one of the most important sculptors of the late nineteenth century. His work is characterized by an innovative freedom of form.

Page 26:
William Holman Hunt (London, 1827–1910) was one of the founding painters of the British art movement of the Pre-Raphaelite Brotherhood, which took as their model the fifteenth-century Italian masters.

Page 29:
Henri Guérin (Bruges, 1929–Plaisance-du-Touch, 2009) was a master glassmaker known for his largely abstract creations. His works are featured in over five hundred sites.

Pages 34 and 101:
Lorenzo di Cione, known as Lorenzo Ghiberti (Florence, 1378–1455) was a sculptor of the Florentine Quattrocento. Along with Donatello, he was one of the initiators of the renewal of modern sculpture.

Page 35:
Duccio di Buoninsegna (Siena, c. 1255/1260–c. 1318/1319) was one of the greatest Sienese painters of his day and the initiator of the International Gothic style.

Page 36:
Michelangelo Merisi da Caravaggio (Milan, 1571–Porto Ercole, 1610) revolutionized seventeenth-century painting and had a profound impact on Western art.

Page 39:
Konrad Witz (Rottweil, c. 1400–Basel, 1445/1446), a painter of Swiss Swabian origin, was among the important late Gothic painters in the upper Rhineland.

Page 45:
Hans Memling (Seligenstadt, c. 1435/1440–Bruges, 1494) was a painter of the Early Netherlandish School and one of the greatest representatives of fifteenth-century Bruges art.

Jacopo Robusti, known as Tintoretto (Venice, 1518–1594), was a Venetian painter of the Renaissance associated with the Mannerist movement. His paintings for the Scuola Grande di San Rocco, have earned it the name of the "Venetian Sistine Chapel."

Page 46:
Agnolo di Cosimo, known as Bronzino (Florence, 1503–1572), was a Florentine Mannerist painter of portraits, religious scenes, and tapestry designs.

Page 47:
Jean-Michel Alberola (born 1953, Saïda, Algeria) lives and works in Paris where, since 1991, he has taught at the city's École supérieure des Beaux-Arts. Painter, sculptor, film-maker, and creator of books and objets d'art, he seeks to unite painting, writing, and the spoken word.

Page 48:
Jacopo Carrucci, known as Pontormo (Pontormo, 1494–Florence, 1557), was an Italian painter of the Florentine School and

one of the most important representatives of the sixteenth-century Mannerist movement in painting.

Page 56:
Domínikos Theotokópoulos, known as El Greco (Héraklion, 1541–Toledo, 1614), a painter, sculptor, and architect, is considered the founding artist of the Spanish School. His painting, a synthesis of Renaissance Mannerism and Byzantine art, is characterized by elongated forms and vivid colors.

William Bouguereau (La Rochelle, 1825–1905) was a French representative of academic painting. After a bereavement suffered in 1877, he turned to religious themes, abandoning the subjects of classical antiquity of his early career.

Page 58:
Rembrandt Harmenszoon van Rijn (Leiden, 1606–Amsterdam, 1669) is generally considered one of the greatest painters of European Baroque art and one of the most important painters of the seventeenth-century Dutch School. Rembrandt also produced etchings and drawings.

Page 65:
Andrea della Robbia (Florence, 1435–1525) was a Florentine ceramist who specialized in glazed terra cotta. He was the founder of the della Robbia studio-workshop where his five sons were trained.

Page 66:
Pieter Fransz de Grebber (Haarlem, c. 1600–1652), a painter, draftsman, and engraver of the Dutch Golden Age, produced principally religious subjects and a treatise on art. He was a pioneer in the field of graphics and was a stylistic innovator.

Page 73:
William Blake (London, 1757–1827) was a British pre-Romantic painter and poet. Known for his watercolors, drawings, engravings, and lithographs, he devoted himself primarily to poetry.

Page 76:
Giotto di Bondone, known as Giotto (Romignano, 1267–Florence, 1337), was an Italian painter, sculptor, and architect of the Trecento whose works were the source of the renewal of Western art. It was the influence of his painting that led to the vast general movement of the Renaissance in the following century.

Page 81:
Tommaso di Giovanni Cassai, known as Masaccio (San Giovanni Valdarno, 1401–Rome, 1428), is considered the greatest painter of the early Italian Renaissance and is traditionally held to be the first painter of the modern age.

Page 83:
Sylvie Gaudin (Boulogne-Billancourt, 1950–1994) was a French artist, painter, and master-glassmaker. She is known for the originality of her stained-glass windows produced in France until her death at the height of her career.

Page 84:
Francesco Borromini, born Francesco Castelli (Bissone, 1599–Rome, 1667), was a prodigious architect of the Baroque period and rival of Bernini. A brilliant artist, he experimented with interpretations of classical themes and handled architectural forms with dynamism.

Michelangelo Buonarotti, known as Michelangelo (Caprese, 1475–Rome, 1564), was a sculptor, painter, architect, poet, and city planner whose work exerted considerable influence on his contemporaries. His "manner" of painting and sculpting was taken up by representatives of what would become known as Mannerism.

Page 92:
Caspar David Friedrich (Greifswald, 1774–Dresden, 1840), a German painter and draftsman, is considered the most significant and influential artist of nineteenth-century German Romantic painting.

Page 94:
Piero della Francesca, born Piero di Benedetto de Franceschi (Borgo San Sepolcro, 1412/1420–1492), was an important figure of the early Italian Renaissance. His artistic body of work is celebrated for its careful study of perspective, the monumental modeling of his subjects, and his expressive use of light.

Page 100:
Bicci di Lorenzo (Florence, 1373–1452), a Florentine proponent of the International Gothic style, came from a long line of painters.

Page 102:
Francisco de Zurbarán (Fuente de Cantos, 1598–Madrid, 1664) was a painter of the Spanish Golden Age. He is famous for his religious paintings, which display great visual power and a profound mysticism.

Page 106:
Francesco Trevisani (Capodistria, 1656–Rome, 1746) was a highly active painter in Rome during what is known as the Rococo period of the Baroque.

Page 110:
Nicolas of Verdun (Verdun, 1130–Tournai, 1205) was a goldsmith who worked near Vienna, in Cologne, and in Tournai. His work marked the transition between the Romanesque and Gothic styles.

Wassily Kandinsky (Moscow, 1866–Neuilly-sur-Seine, 1944), a painter and art theoretician, is considered one of the most important artists of the twentieth century.

Page 113:
Joseph Mallord William Turner (London, 1775–Chelsea, 1851) was a painter, watercolorist, and engraver whose work is marked by an innovative style earned him the reputation as "the painter of light."

Page 118:
Hieronymus van Aken, known as Hieronymus Bosch (Bois-le-Duc, c. 1450–1516), a member of the Brotherhood of Our Lady, was a Netherlandish painter whose work mingles heaven and hell, satire and morality.

Page 119:
Alfred Manessier (Saint-Ouen, 1911–Orléans, 1993), a non-figurative artist keen on the interpretation of nature, is considered one of the masters of the New School of Paris.

Page 121:
Éric Michel was born in Aix-en-Provence in 1962. His work, in particular his paintings of pure saturated pigment, his videos, and creations in fluorescent light, fall within the tradition of the quest for the immaterial.

Page 126:
Auguste Gilbert Privat (Toulouse, 1892–Soulac-sur-Mer, 1969), a French sculptor and painter, was awarded the Prix de Rome in 1921.

Giovanni di Paolo (Siena, 1399 or 1403–1482) was a manuscript illuminator and painter of the early Sienese Renaissance whose style was influenced by Gothic art.

Back Cover:
Jean Malouel (Nijmegen, Netherlands, before 1370–Dijon, France, 1416) was painter to the Duke of Burgundy from 1397 until his death. He executed this *Pièta* around the year 1400.

Index of Prayers, Poems, and Hymns

Art Credits

Cover: Fra Angelico, *Christ Giving His Blessing*, Musée du Louvre, Paris, France. © RMN-Grand Palais (Musée du Louvre) / Gérard Blot.

Page 4: Novgorod School, *First Council of Nicea in the Presence of Constantine the Great in 325*, Palazzo Leoni-Montanari, Vicenza, Italy. © The Art Archive / G. Dagli Orti.

Page 7: *Angel Musician Playing the Organ*, Musée des Augustins, Toulouse, France. © Hervé Champollion / akg-images.

Page 9: Master Honoré (imitator of), *The Apostles' Creed*, miniature from *la Somme le Roi*, ms. 0870, f. 005, Bibliothèque Mazarine, Paris, France. © Bibliothèque Mazarine, Paris.

Page 13: Girolamo dai Libri, *God the Father with His Hand Raised in Blessing*, National Gallery of Art, Washington D.C., USA. © Courtesy National Gallery of Art, Washington.

Pages 14-15: Philippe de Champaigne, *God the Father Creating the Material Universe*, Musée des Beaux-Arts, Rouen, France. © The Bridgeman Art Library.

Pages 16-17: Maurice Denis, *Young Girls and Angels*, panel from *Eternal Spring*, Musée départemental Maurice Denis, Saint-Germain-en-Laye, France. © 2013, ADAGP.

Pages 18-19: *The Dome of the Creation*, San Marco Basilica, Venice, Italy. © Cameraphoto Arte Venezia / The Bridgeman Art Library.

Page 21: Auguste Rodin, *The Hand of God* or *Creation*, Musée Rodin, Paris, France. © Musée Rodin, Paris. Cliché Christian Baraja.

Page 23: *Christ in Majesty Surrounded by Symbols of the Evangelists*, Musée de Cluny, Paris, France. © RMN-Grand Palais (Musée de Cluny - Musée national du Moyen-Âge) / Gérard Blot.

Page 24: *The Wissembourg Head of Christ*, stained glass from the former abbey of Wissembourg, Musée de l'Œuvre de Notre-Dame, Strasbourg, France. © The Bridgeman Art Library.

Page 27: William Holman Hunt, *The Light of the World*, Keble College, Oxford, United Kingdon. © IAM / akg-images.

Pages 28-29: *The Son Enthroned*, Commentary on the Psalms, Petrus Lombardus, fol. 185, initial O of Psalm 109, Bibliothèque Sainte-Geneviève, Paris, France. © Bibliothèque Sainte-Geneviève, Paris. Cliché IRHT.

Pages 30-31: Henri Guérin, *Bursts of Gold*, Musée de Verre, Conches, France. © Didier Taillefer.

Page 33: Lorenzo Ghiberti, *The Annunciation*, Florence, Italy. © Photo Scala, Florence.

Pages 34-35: Duccio di Buoninsegna, *The Nativity*, National Gallery of Art, Washington D.C., USA. © De Agostini / akg-images.

Page 37: Michelangelo Merisi da Caravaggio, *The Madonna of Loreto*, Church of Sant'Agostino, Rome, Italy. © Photo Scala, Florence.

Page 38: Youhannès de Berkri (Vaspurakan), *The Baptism of Christ*, from an Armenian Manuscript, Armenian Museum, Isfahan, Iran. © The Art Archive / Armenian Museum Isfahan / Dagli Orti.

Pages 40-41: Konrad Witz, *The Decision of the Redemption*, Gemäldegalerie, Berlin, Germany. © BPK, Berlin, dist. RMN / Grand Palais / Jörg P. Anders.

Page 43: Hans Memling, *The Virgin Presenting the Man of Sorrows*, Museum of the Royal Chapel, Granada, Spain. © Photo Scala, Florence.

Page 44: Tintoretto, *Christ before Pilate*, Scuola Grande di San Rocco, Venice, Italy. © Photo Scala, Florence.

Page 46: Bronzino, *The Crucifixion*, Musée des Beaux-Arts, Nice, France. © Ville de Nice. Photo Muriel Anssens.

Page 47: Jean-Michel Albérola, *The Sacred Heart*, Comité national d'art sacré, Paris, France. © 2013, ADAGP.

Page 48: Jacopo Pontormo, *The Deposition*, Church of Santa Felicità, Florence, Italy. © akg-images / Rabatti-Domingie.

Pages 50-51: The Master of Chaource, *The Entombment*, Church of Saint-Jean-Baptiste, Chaource, France. © Jean-François Amelot / La Collection.

Page 53: *The Holy Women at the Tomb*, Sées Cathedral, France. © Francis Bouquerel.

Page 54: Domínikos Theotokópoulos, known as El Greco, *The Resurrection*, Spain. © akg-images / Erich Lessing.

Page 57: William Adolphe Bouguereau, *The Holy Women at the Tomb*, Koninklijk Museum voor Schone Kunsten, Anvers, Belgium © Lukas - Art in Flanders VZW / Photo Hugo Maertens / The Bridgeman Art Library.

Pages 58-59: Rembrandt, *Christ and the Two Disciples on the Road to Emmaus*, Musée du Louvre, Paris, France. © RMN-Grand Palais (Musée du Louvre) / Thierry Le Mage.

Pages 60-61: Fra Angelico, *Noli me tangere*, Florence, Museum of the Convent of San Marco, Italy. © Photo Scala, Florence - courtesy of the Ministero Beni e Att. Culturali.

Page 63: *The Ascension*, Musée de Cluny, Paris, France. © RMN-Grand Palais (Musée de Cluny - Musée national du Moyen-Âge) /Jean-Gilles Berizzi.

Page 65: Andrea della Robbia, *The Ascension of Christ*, Chiesa Maggiore, La Verna, Italy. © Photo Scala, Florence.

Pages 66-67: Pieter de Grebber, *God Invites Christ to Be Seated on the Throne at His Right Hand*, Museum Cartharijneconvent, Utrecht. © akg-images.

Pages 68-69: *Triptych of the Trinity*, Musée national de la Renaissance, Écouen, France. © RMN-Grand Palais (Musée de la Renaissance, château d'Écouen) / René-Gabriel Ojéda.

Page 71: *The Last Judgment*, illumination from *Psalter of Ingeborg of Denmark*, Musée Condé, Chantilly, France. © The Bridgeman Art Library.

Page 73: William Blake, *Christ Accepting the Office of Redeemer*, Museum of Fine Arts, Boston, Massachusetts, USA. © Photographer © 2013, Museum of Fine Arts, Boston.

Pages 74-75: *The Last Judgment*, west porch tympanum, Abbey of Sainte-Foy, Conques, France. © Jean-Paul Dumontier / La Collection.

Page 77: Giotto di Bondone, *Christ Pantocrator*, vault detail, Scrovegni Chapel, Padua, Italy. © akg-images / Mportfolio / Electa.

Page 79: *The Holy Spirit*, Church of Santo Domingo, Puebla, Mexico. © The Art Archive / A. Dagli Orti.

Page 80: Masaccio, *The Trinity*, Church of Santa Maria Novella, Florence, Italy. © Alinari Archives, Florence. Dist. RMN-Grand Palais / Georges Tatge.

Pages 82-83: Sylvie Gaudin, *Pentecost*, Church of Saint-Gervais, Paris, France. © The Art Archive / G. Dagli Orti. © Ateliers Gaudin, Paris.

Pages 84-85: Borromini, *Dome*, Church of San Carlo alle Quattro Fontane, Rome, Italy. © Andrea Jemolo / Scala, Florence.

Pages 86-87: Michelangelo, *Ezekiel*, Sistine Chapel, Vatican, Italy. © Alinari Archives, Florence. Dist. RMN-Grand Palais / Georges Tatge.

Page 89: The Master of Cabestany, *The Appearance of Christ to Two Disciples*, Frederic Marès Museum, Barcelona, Spain. © Museu Frederic Marès / Photo : Ramon Muro.

Pages 90-91: Greek School, *The Holy Apostles Peter and Paul*, Louvre Museum, Paris, France. © RMN-Grand Palais (Musée du Louvre) /Jean-Gilles Berizzi.

Page 93: Caspar David Friedrich, *The Cathedral*, Georg Schäfer Museum, Schweinfurt, Germany. © Artothek / La Collection.

Page 94: Piero della Francesca, *The Madonna of Mercy*, central panel of the *Polyptych of the Misericordia*, Museo Civico, Sansepolcro, Italy. © akg-images / Erich Lessing.

Pages 96-97: Roman School, *View of Saint Peter's Square in Rome*, Galleria Sabauda, Turin, Italy. © Archives Alinari, Florence, dist. RMN-Grand Palais / Mauro Magliani.

Page 99: Bicci di Lorenzo, The Baptism of Saint Pancras, Bandini Museum, Fiesole, Italy. © Photo Scala, Florence.

Pages 100-101: Lorenzo Ghiberti, *The Gates of Paradise*, bronze, east door, Baptistery of Saint John, Florence, Italy. © Photo Scala, Florence.

Page 103: Baptistery, Saint-Sauveur Cathedral, Aix-en-Provence, France. © Giraudon / The Bridgeman Art Library.

Pages 104-105: Francisco de Zurbarán, *Agnus Dei*, Prado Musem, Madrid, Spain. © Photo Scala, Florence.

Page 107: Francesco Trevisani, *Peter Baptizes Cornelius the Centurion*, private collection. © Photo Christie's Images / The Bridgeman Art Library.

Page 109: Nicolas of Verdun, *The Resurrection of the Dead*, detail of the altar, Abbey Church of Klosterneuburg, Austria. © akg-images / Erich Lessing.

Page 111: Wassily Kandinsky, *The Last Judgment*. © Sotheby's / akg-images.

Pages 112-113: The Mausoleum of Galla Placidia, Ravenna, Italy. © akg-images / Cameraphoto.

Pages 114-115: Joseph Mallord William Turner, *The Angel Standing in the Sun*, (c. 1846), Tate Collection, London, Great Britain. © Tate, London, dist. RMN-Grand Palais / Tate Photography.

Page 117: *The Good Shepherd*, Pio Cristiano Museum, Vatican, Italy. © Photo Scala, Florence.

Page 118: Hieronymus Bosch, *Ascent to the Empyrean*, panel from the *Altarpiece of the Last Judgment*, late 11th century. © Artothek / La Collection.

Page 120: *The Vision of the Heavenly Jerusalem*, Bibliothèque nationale de France, Paris. © BnF.

Page 121: Éric Michel, *Infinity*. © 2013, ADAGP.

Pages 122-123: Alfred Manessier, *Alleluia*, Musée Boucher de Perthes, Abbeville, France. © RMN-Grand Palais / Thierry Ollivier. © 2013, ADAGP.

Page 125: Auguste Gilbert Privat, *The Prayer*, Private Collection. © The Bridgeman Art Library. © Right Reserved.

Page 127: Giovanni di Paolo, *Paradise* (detail), The Metropolitan Museum of Art, New York, NY, USA. © The Metropolitan Museum of Art, dist. RMN-Grand Palais / image of the MMA.

Back cover: Jean Malouel, T*he Mercy of Our Lord*, or *The Great Round Pietà*, Musée du Louvre, Paris, France. © RMN-Grand Palais (Musée du Louvre) /Jean-Gilles Berizzi.

Printed in August 2013 by Donnelley, Mexico
Edition number: MNG13011
www.magnificat.com